GOD IS YOUR FATHER

God is your Father
Copyright © 2022 by Marcus Newsome

Published in the United States of America

ISBN   Paperback: 978-1-958030-74-5
ISBN   eBook: 978-1-958030-75-2

All rights reserved. No part of this publication may be reproduced, stored in a retrieval system or transmitted in any way by any means, electronic, mechanical, photocopy, recording or otherwise without the prior permission of the author except as provided by USA copyright law.

The opinions expressed by the author are not necessarily those of ReadersMagnet, LLC.

ReadersMagnet, LLC
10620 Treena Street, Suite 230 | San Diego, California, 92131 USA
1.619. 354. 2643 | www.readersmagnet.com

Book design copyright © 2022 by ReadersMagnet, LLC. All rights reserved.

Cover design by Kent Gabutin
Interior design by Daniel Lopez

GOD IS YOUR FATHER

Marcus Newsome

ReadersMagnet, LLC

I would like to dedicate this Book to my MOM, Bernice Woolridge Newsome, who is in Heaven. The one who Taught me to pray. GOD gave me a Vision of you in the Bosom of JESUS with two angels on each side flying up to Heaven. And three weeks later you went Home. Thank you, MOM, for instilling the most Valuable Asset to Connect with GOD. PRAYER

EARTHLY AUTHORITIES AND GOD

All ordinances of man must be according to the laws of GOD, or it is not an ordinance of GOD. GOD is always the same, and all His laws and commands are in Exodus 20. Specifically, this verse: "Thou shall not kill." There was nothing said after that, just "don't kill." In other words, anything that is not worthy of death. There are crimes that are not worthy of death, and if one is killed anyway, it becomes murder. If you submit to this one verse in obedience to GOD, then you are under His authority, and He is obligated to protect you. Listen to His position of authority that was given to him because of his obedience to GOD. "All power has been given unto me in Heaven and in Earth" (Matthew 28:18). Now Jesus says "All power," and nothing is left out. That means the president, all judges, all police officials, and every authority in between are to subject themselves to GOD, and they must submit to Him according to His commands.

Every law goes back to GOD who (get this) destroyed death and the one who had the power of death, who is the devil. So if He destroyed death, then death is not in His plan, not as far as executing it under His authorities when law enforcement execute death outside of defense—they do it under human authority, not GOD's. Ordained authority of GOD does not mean that whatever they decide, GOD agrees and is behind it. They can disobey GOD and bring judgment to themselves just as well as a civilian.

If GOD was behind every decision that any authority made, then when a judge passed a law, giving the right for a man to marry a man, and in their thinking that GOD agrees, and our ministers have GOD's blessing and the power of His spirit to perform the ceremony, GOD forbid. If we agree with same-sex marriage, then why not agree with rape and theft? You see, this is the way the GOD of the Bible operates. Once He brings together a duty, He expects it to function just the way He put it together, and His spirit and power does not assist it because it's not His idea, and when one does not see and function just the way GOD says, then that makes it sin. Not once did GOD, even with not one sin, no, not one. What GOD is trying to avoid in our lives is death because sin brings death because of the absence of GOD, and the Bible states that GOD is not the GOD of the dead, but of the living (Luke 20:38). So everyone that has died, GOD had no hand in it. But everyone that is alive, GOD had a hand in sustaining that life, depending on the submission of authority, and everyone that lives forever will be because of Him. That's His plan (life).

Talking about the ordinance of man, let me take you to a passage that explains this meaning because it's not just talking about law enforcement. Let's read first, then we will go back and pull truth from what we have read. "Submit yourselves to every ordinance of man, for the Lord's sake" (1 Peter 2:13). First of all, submission should be for the Lord's sake and nothing else. In other words, because He is watching, you will obey. Then it goes on to say who to submit to, whether it be to kings (president) as supreme or unto governors, as unto them that are sent by Him for punishment of evildoers and for praise of them that do well. These are those who seek to not break the law.

No man can ever be under the authority of GOD without mercy. Mercy is where officials find every means necessary to make you better by working with your willingness to work with them. Looking over weaknesses because even in the office of authority, we make mistakes and we also want to be overlooked. So here is how it goes with GOD! When we don't overlook weaknesses and sins, our weaknesses and sins will not be overlooked. In other words, an official receives punishment for their shortcomings and wrongdoings. When you don't forgive, then you will not be forgiven; when you don't show mercy to others, then GOD will not show mercy to you (James 2:13).

So therefore, the spirit of GOD's protection is not with officials who don't show mercy and not overall looking to a person's well-being. When it is put in the mind of a police officer to rush to a scene to just kill to make an example through death (guess what?), that's what they will receive in return. Not saying that they shouldn't go to a scene and kill because sometimes it takes them to kill in order to stop a killer. If the chief of law enforcement thinks that murder delivers a message that keeps criminals from crime, he is wrong. When a criminal loses his life because of his crime, it must be under the message of GOD's judgment and point to GOD. Man's judgment shows a heart of murder and points to man. But in GOD's agenda to show mercy, this also shows the judgment of GOD, and only the criminals get the message that delivers the right fear (the fear of GOD). However, the fear of man generates anger, not only in criminals, but also the public, and it drives them into a vengeance type of spirit because of the absence of GOD's spirit, which speaks to all men, even evil men.

Only GOD can deliver the right message to men and women of crime. Let me put it to you this way that will give you a natural understanding. We all had fathers and mothers as children. Some good, some bad. But what happens to a young child in the raising from his parents, that as an ongoing, good father who has been showing love all along?

Talk about the spirit of GOD because GOD is love. So in the chastening of that father, He fusses at him about a mistake, but yet treats him with respect. So then that child can see the heart of his father who wants him to do better and in the way GOD wired us humans. He can truly see GOD himself. This kind of love opens the child's heart to his or her dad and has a place in that child's heart that no one else has.

I'm still on authorities of GOD and how they must distribute GOD Himself and not themselves. Only then does that child get the right understanding of authority, and in right distribution of GOD, that child, in his mind, grabs hold of GOD correctly through design and now has a place for the correct fear to be deposited. Fear that doesn't bring anger. Fear that doesn't generate vengeance, but reverence. Well, it's still the same with men of age. When a person is being pressured into something without an inner understanding of GOD's love, it doesn't bring correction, but anger. GOD's method never changes because GOD doesn't change.

Here is the bottom line about GOD and the authority that He ordains. There should be a fear of GOD and a submission to His agenda to maintain the lives of men hoping for repentance. That's why He is waiting to come back. That's why He delivers mercy (undeserved favor). GOD's hope is that all men turn from wickedness, and His hope is that every man enters heaven. We can strengthen His hope or destroy the process through illegitimacy. "The Lord is not slack concerning His promise as some men count slackness: but is long suffering to us-ward, not willing that any should perish, but that all should come to repentance" (2 Peter 3:9).

The word *long-suffering* defined is this: Having or showing patience in spite of troubles, especially those caused by other people. When man does not consider GOD's agenda, he can't say that he is under the authority of GOD's ordinances.

HOW JUDGMENT FALLS ON LAW ENFORCEMENT

Now let me show you from GOD's word how judgment falls on any authority. When they step between men and women of GOD, who carries the saving message of Jesus Christ? No authority has the right to tamper with human rights to obey GOD. Back in the Old Testament, there were authorities that commanded the apostles not to preach in the name of Jesus. They hated the fact that the apostles were taking the reverence from them and directing it to Jesus, or so it seemed. But listen to what the Holy Spirit rose up in one of the apostles and said, "We ought to obey GOD rather than man" (Acts 5:29).

A person who lacks understanding would think that this would not be submitting to the ordinance of man, but as GOD puts it, no authority has the right to command you to disobey GOD.

There was a man named Gamaliel who experienced past judgments that was falling on men of authority. It was the fact that they were ignorantly working against GOD and fighting His plan of salvation to get men into heaven. In this passage of scripture, focus on the fact that the men that were driving the people as head authority were the ones losing their lives. In other words, listen to how Gamaliel focuses on leadership.

"At this, the high council was furious and decided to kill the Apostles. But one member had a different perspective. He was a Pharisee named Gamaliel, who was an expert on religious law and was very popular with the people. He stood up and ordered that the apostles be sent outside the council chamber for a while. Then he addressed his colleagues as follows: Men of Israel, take care what you are planning to do to these men! Some time ago there was that fellow Theudas, who pretended to be someone great. About four hundred others joined him, but he was killed and his followers went their various ways. The whole movement came to nothing. After him, at the time of the Census, there was Judas of Galilea. He got some people to follow him, but he was killed too, and his followers were scattered. So my advice is, leave these men alone. If they are doing this merely on their own, it will soon be overthrown [because no power of the Holy Spirit]. But if it is of GOD, you will not be able to stop them. You may even find yourself fighting against GOD" (Acts 5:33–39, NLT). Now here is where it gets tricky for authorities because the Holy Spirit is not like man, because a person does not have to be distinguished for him to dwell and operate. Jesus gave a command to His children to go into all the world and preach the gospel everywhere (Mark 1b:15). Now the Holy Spirit dwells in schoolteachers, janitors, ditch diggers, loggers, lawyers, and talk-show hosts. This command should make any authority be aware that GOD can be in any man that claims Jesus and that human rights cannot be hindered. Not just because one has a church or congregation, but also ordinary civilians. Anywhere judgment falls is where you seek to stop progress of GOD's Spirit and what He has rights to. There is a growing demand to pass more laws today to protect law enforcement. To me, they are viewing the issue one-sided. In a godly agenda, law enforcement should be protected. But should men and women be killed by police officers, men whose actions were not worthy of death, because in GOD's eyes that's murder. Murder, where a life was taken that may not have been prepared for heaven, so then GOD loses. So now we understand why the Father operates through Jesus His Son only, who distributes mercy and grace (favor underserved). If it is favor underserved, then you receive it even when you weren't supposed to, and you may ask, how exactly does this benefit GOD? Well, let's understand something. If GOD gave His Son to die for the world (John 3:1b), that means GOD gave Him to die for that vagabond that lives under the bridge. You may not think he is valuable, but he is valuable to GOD, and any soul that is taken without Jesus is a soul that has been won by Satan and lost by GOD. And it is a soul that could have been won if actions toward him were proper and given a reason to love back.

Let's look at GOD's heart and you will find an understanding of how He operates with you and me. What should be in the purpose of our prayers when we pray for all that are in authority? It is not for our selfishness, but to accomplish heaven's desire. In other words, it is for God's plan to work through our leadership in cooperation, because the plan can waver from GOD to Satan according to the spirit of our prayers that we, the church, pray upon our authorities. "I exhort therefore, that first of all supplications, prayers and intersessions and thanks be made for all men; for King's [president] and for all that are in authority; that we may lead a quiet and peaceable life in all Godliness and honesty. For this is good and acceptable in the sight of GOD, our Savior; who will have all men to be saved and come to the knowledge of truth" (1 Timothy 2:1–4). In GOD's agenda, He wants us to function in a way that gives men a chance to be saved and come to know the truth that changes their hearts. This is why mercy is important. According to how we pray toward our leaders is how they respond to us and our people. In that verse, it says supplications. This means that we supply GOD in our prayers the correct heart for souls. Then He releases the power of the Holy Spirit and the fear of GOD upon authorities and turns their hearts to His plans.

Why would He even say "Pray for them"? So overall, it's not the authorities that are going to give us a peaceful and quiet life, it's GOD. When we turn from our wicked ways, GOD delivers power to the land and work through men and women, but when we neglect mercy and pray prayers of vengeance, GOD's plan is ignored and lives are lost. Authorities are murdered and even church leadership is judged. And now, verse 5 shows us how our prayers are accomplished with GOD to all men, "There is one mediator between GOD and man, the man Christ Jesus."

HEAVEN AND EARTHLY GOVERNMENT

Remember this one thing: GOD uses us all to help each other in human government. There is human government and there is heaven's government. Keep in mind of these two governments and you will understand heaven's function and earth's function. The word *govern* means to "exercise continuous sovereign authority over." If you belong to heaven, then heaven's government (Jesus Christ) should be in sovereign authority over your life. If you are not submitted to the government of heaven, then you are not in full protection of heaven. Don't be deceived; obedience to GOD is more of a protection than earthly government. Earthly government should be secondary. If you encounter danger, Earthly Authorities got to get there to protect you. But GOD knew that you were going to be in danger that very day when you were in your mother's womb. GOD the Father is grieved when He is not first and when you don't truly depend on Him as Father. The danger for us is that if we put any man in front of GOD, then GOD has no other choice but to let your beliefs work for you, and whoever is first in your life is truly your GOD. Never make any man your god. Every authority of GOD must be in its proper order. "And GOD commanded us to submit to [every] ordinance of man" (1 Peter 2:13). The definition for ordinance: "A law set forth by government authorities, a decree or direction." One way you can tell that GOD is speaking from heaven when He brings judgment on even authority figures is when they seek to use their force against GOD-given human rights. No authority figure has any right to keep you from human rights.

If you are in authority, there are other authorities that you submit to that are in a different field than your authority. A police officer himself is ordered by GOD to submit to different authorities other than his. Remember that GOD said "every ordinance of man." But overall, authority is GOD Himself, and He has set forth heaven's authorities that speak and show signs that GOD is speaking from heaven.

HOLY SPIRIT

First, I want to make you understand some things about the Holy Spirit. The Bible talks about fruit. In our human senses, GOD used the understanding of how we feel when we encounter fruit. Very sweet and pleasant to enjoy and eat when it is ripe. Growing as people of GOD, your fruit can be bitter for lack of ripeness. That doesn't mean that you aren't doing what GOD requires, but it's just that your actions toward others haven't reached its full potential.

With this understanding, it will show you where you are when it comes to the fruit of GOD's Spirit. The Holy Spirit is GOD's Spirit. The day that a person is born again, GOD gives you His Spirit, who is to be your guide. You become a new believer, but that doesn't mean that you will never make another mistake. You will make mistakes, but now you have a Spirit that leads you to function like a child of GOD. No person of GOD should be under another spirit but GOD's Spirit, and like the understanding of fruit, everything about Him distributes pleasure or grace to others. The Bible states that by your fruit is how you are known (Matthew 7). So, in other words, to distinguish between spirits is how that person is treating the other. If in doing something toward another person, no matter what it is, there is a spirit that is in operation, whether it's a human spirit or demonic spirit, a worldly spirit or GOD's Spirit.

But now get this: The only one that cannot be judged is GOD's Spirit. His purpose is always to bring love, joy, and peace always to give faith (know him). "But the fruit of the Spirit is 'Love'" (Galatians 5:22).

Notice the word *love* is first and foremost. His first motive is love. GOD is love, and if GOD is love, then all His actions are to love, joy, peace, long suffering, gentle, goodness (verse 22). When you allow GOD's Spirit, you are always gentle and good, faithful (verse 22). The Holy Spirit gives us faith to distribute to the better of others. That's if you depend on Him. All these come from Him. If you are not distributing these to all people, even your enemy, then you are not allowing GOD's Spirit to flow—meekness, temperance (verse 22).

Now listen to what it says right at the end of this verse, "Against such there is no law." That means that GOD has set no law in action to hinder you from distributing these fruits. And if someone commands you not to, then that person is not under the authority of GOD, because GOD the Holy Spirit longs for each of us to become ripe in this fruit.

When I first became a believer, for some strange reason, in my innocence, some people began to attack my presence and I sought GOD about these attacks. Do you know what He said? "Now that you are my child and have denounced other spirits." That's why Jesus was attacked in his ministry because evil spirits recognized Him as the Son of GOD through his submission to the Holy Spirit Only and His rejection to all other spirits. No one had to tell them; they know because you no longer give them authority to act through you. This is how we become a spectacle or light, because your actions are different, and in your actions, some people see you as weak because you return good for their ugly. You allow GOD and not you, but you become a powerful being because it's GOD who is acting, not us. These attacks are what ripens your fruit, because as the Spirit flows in a continuous pace, He ripens your actions of fruit. The Spirit is there to help us become better, and we need to learn how to tap into the Spirit. There may be someone in your life whom you feel you shouldn't be good to or be patient with. Something in us doesn't want to, but then we make a conscious decision to call Him to work. There is something about the Spirit where He tells us when we are right or wrong, and it's called conviction. And when we are convicted, He gives us a right to choose GOD or yourself (obey Him). He only convicts us because He loves us.

GOD IS YOUR FATHER

Do you know that the Son of GOD was tempted to kill? Of course, GOD the Father gave Him the right to choose, but He chose to yield to the Spirit and always receive strength from the Spirit to reject His evil desires. Everything that temps us, Jesus was tempted at all points. The Holy Spirit is there to maintain righteousness.

UNSTOPPABLE

When you operate by GOD's Spirit, you are unstoppable because your faith is in GOD and your desires have been cast down and is no longer you but GOD Himself. And every time you walk into a room, all other spirits know you because GOD is sovereign or in control. The Spirit in you is greater than the spirit in this world. That's not boasting about you, but GOD. Any evil that rises in order to stop your spiritual actions is summoned to GOD's judgments and is destroyed. There is no law against such when we function from the Spirit. We need to get to the point to where we take GOD at His word; we can't have our own agenda when it comes to the truth of His word. Cast down anything that is contrary against truth. The Holy Spirit is speaking to you. Depend on GOD 100 percent, and you will see the power of GOD. The more you are tempted and you reject, the more powerful the Holy Spirit becomes in you. If Jesus had not rejected sin, He would not have been as powerful as He was even though He is the Son of GOD, because by yielding to sin, you give up GOD and your power becomes diluted. That's how the Spirit works. Every time you obey, your Spirit gets stronger; every time you disobey, you Spirit becomes weaker, and this goes for all humanity. The anointing of GOD should be important to you. In obedience, the Holy Spirit knows how to unite to your Spirit and give you clarity, but when the Spirit is grieved, your clarity is diluted. (Maintain your first love for GOD.)

FINANCIAL GIVING

In this part, we will see how your giving adds the power of the Spirit and cultivates eternal life with GOD. Your first love for GOD only means that you put GOD first in all you do, and trust me, GOD knows what this world offers that has a hold on our hearts, and it's our money. When we go to work, from morning to afternoon, all those hours are to bring finances to our pockets and many other things we do in life. GOD has given you a choice to prove your love for Him by supporting His work, and every time you support the work of GOD, you are strengthening the Spirit of eternal life in your life. Your teachers should be supported, those who distribute the Spirit-filled words to you. Let's go to GOD's word, and we will see how this process works in Galatians 6:6–10. Notice that we will read this line upon line, meaning that the part we start from will be first, and all after that will be talking about the first verse we started. "Let Him who is, taught in word communicate to him that teaches in all good things" (verse 6). Now let me read that from the New Living Translation, "Those who are taught the word of GOD should help their teachers by paying them." "The truth of GOD's word" means when you help your teachers, you are obeying GOD and adding eternal life by cultivating your Spirit (line upon line). Be not deceived, GOD is not mocked.

Remember, He is still talking about verse 6: "For whatsoever a man soweth, [that] shall he also reap. For he that soweth to his flesh, shall of the flesh reap corruption, but he that soweth to the Spirit, shall of the Spirit reap everlasting life." That means that if you are being given information from GOD's word and don't help your teacher, you are sowing to your flesh and corrupting your knowledge of GOD. But when you help your teachers, you are sowing to the Holy Spirit, and He cultivates eternal life. So, here, GOD is supporting those that teach you everlasting life. That's what the Bible says, so we have to take GOD at His word. Obeying these verses is obeying the Spirit of GOD Himself, and this strengthens your anointing and clarity of truth. Trust me when I say that you are adding power to your life because you are connecting yourself to the knowledge of your teacher.

Our beliefs bring power and authority to our lives. We will receive our external life at the right time, as it says in verse 9 to 10. The Holy Spirit is drawing you to Jesus and the knowledge of Him through your support of His work. How and what you sow is how and what you reap. "I say unto you, He which soweth sparingly shall reap also sparingly; and He which soweth bountifully, shall also reap bountifully" (2 Corinthians 9:6). That means how you believe GOD is how you get from GOD. There is protection when you obey GOD because your anointing becomes strong, and the power of God acts as a force field. The life-giver strengthens you and adds life. Ananias and his wife, Sapphira, lied to GOD about giving and the Spirit of life departed (Acts 5, GOD loves a cheerful giver), as it says in 2 Corinthians 9:7–9. Now here is what it says at the end of verse 9, "And His righteousness remains forever." This means that when you give to GOD's work cheerfully or, in other words, just for the love of God with Him only on your heart, your righteousness remains forever. Believe it or not, the power of the Holy Spirit goes with what you give. Let me ask you this, who are you ultimately in obedience to? GOD, not man, so therefore everything that GOD commands carries His Spirit and makes it holy. This is the reason Ananias and his wife lost their lives when they disrespected GOD, thinking they were getting over on a man. They didn't understand the fact that what they were doing was spiritual and not humanistic.

Because our giving carries blessings, or not giving carries curses through disobedience or lack of reverence to GOD; because if the scriptures tell you to give and you don't, this is what the Bible calls unbelief, which is defined as one very fact: you don't believe GOD! When you truly believe GOD, you do what he says. And as long as you are in subjection to GOD, then His Spirit gives clarity, which brings us to a direct focus.

FOCUS

Every man and woman must keep focus. Not only to GOD's word, but also His plan for our lives individually. Because GOD's plan for your life has been deposited in your heart by GOD Himself. This one thing I know is that GOD calls many of His children after showing themselves proved unto GOD. But that person, and only that person, can really take that calling and bring it to focus, whether it be a disc jockey, doctor, schoolteacher, or street preacher, just to name a few. But you and only you know what drives you and makes you joyful when you do it.

I know that calling our Father has designed a system through being led by the Spirit that guides you to the very place where He has called you to be. Now listen to what Jesus said in a word, letting us know that being focused on the leadership of the Holy Spirit must be in the process and eventually lead you to success. This simple fact is that if you're being led by the Spirit, then you are being led by Jesus and the Father. "Peter asked Jesus, 'What will we get if we leave everyone else's plan for our lives and pursue GOD's plan for our lives?' [Which is always for the Gospel.] And He answered and said, 'I assure you [which means it will happen], there is no man who has left houses or brothers or sisters or father or mother or wife or children or lands, for my sake and the Gospels, who will receive in return in this life, a hundred times over—houses, brothers, sisters, mothers, children and property—with persecutions'" (Mark 10:28–31).

I asked myself, you mean to tell me that persecutions come with hundredfold blessings? Believe it or not, persecutions are what keeps your focus and need to remain in Christ. These are haters, those that are jealous. It is a spirit of the world that can sense your righteous spirit by lack of subjection to it. And it persecutes those who have the Spirit of GOD, the same spirit that persecuted Christ, and some foes may come from your own family members and friends. What gets me is that some persecutions come from people that know nothing about you, that get their information from gossip or their own mind. Now you see why the Spirit of GOD is so important so that He can maintain your spiritual walk with the Him and help us continue to love those that persecute us.

When we love, it keeps GOD on our side and His Holy Spirit at work on the hearts of those we encounter. This, my friend, is the Spirit of Jesus when we continue to love those who bring pain and trouble. If you happen to be hurt by someone, the first thing you must do is maintain focus to forgive that person. The minute you do, you keep that connection with your Father GOD, and He grants all your requests according to His will. Sometimes Satan uses people or our selfish desires to lure our focus away from GOD through offerings where we disobey GOD to achieve. That's how we know it is not GOD.

There was a time when Satan came to tempt Jesus. It was the Holy Spirit that led him to be tempted by Satan. It was a test of GOD. GOD never leads us into temptation, but He leads us to be tempted. There is a difference. It was part of GOD's plan for Him to be tempted and is what I call a power test. Worldly power or the power of the Holy Spirit. "Then Jesus was led up of the Spirit to be tempted in the wilderness of the Devil. And when he had fasted forty days and forty nights, He was afterwards hungered" (Matthew 4:1–2).

Before we continue, keep in mind that GOD sent Him to die in our place, and the same temptation that Adam and Eve failed is now at the Son of GOD. This is also a test to maintain GOD as His Father, and what did He do? Every time He was tempted, He refused. There were three answers He gave Satan. All three revered to His Father and your Father. Verse 4 is written, "Man shall not live by bread alone," (stating that not only food keeps you alive, but obedience to GOD's word keeps His Spirit of life). He goes on to say, "But by every word that proceedeth out of the mouth of GOD" (verse 10). "Get thee hence, Satan: for it is written, thou shalt worship the

Lord thy GOD, and Him only shalt thou serve." Jesus resisted, and verse 11 says, "Then the Devil leaveth Him. The reason I carried you through His rejections of Satan was this very fact that He kept GOD as His Father and maintained the full power of the Holy Spirit." *Glory to GOD.*

MARRIAGE AND DIVORCE

First, let's talk about marriage. You can never talk about marriage or the functions of marriage unless you go to the one who first ordained marriage. Marriage was brought about for what I see as just two reasons. First, GOD was looking to give man satisfaction. As wise as GOD is, He was looking into the future of man and what will be needed because He knew that man needed someone like Him to satisfy His needs. After all, GOD is a spirit and man is a spirit also, but has flesh. GOD was in the helping mood to bring about an intimate relationship, so GOD created the relationship and created the woman. That's why it says "Bone of my bone and flesh of my flesh." Fleshly speaking, the man was alone. When we talk about wisdom, we mention GOD's words and He says this: "It is not good that man shall be alone. I will make him a helper comparable to him."

That one word that GOD spoke sums up the whole deal as far as satisfying his aloneness. That word *comparable* means "admitting of comparison with another or others or similar or equivalent." In other words: equal.

Now we have the man with an equal partner: the woman, and now he can say, "I have someone like me, which the flesh had to be completely satisfied as far as relations to GOD, through GOD Himself becoming flesh." We will talk on that later.

The second reason was for GOD Himself to bring forth more humans to fill the earth. Now you have marriage and the function of marriage, which is so wonderful when it operates as GOD ordained. The most important function of marriage or any other relationship is that the two become one. The man and the woman.

One thing that is overlooked and misunderstood is that once the man and woman touch each other sexually, they become one, as far as flesh is concerned. This is where GOD ordains marriage. When a man and woman agree to be together for life, they have sex and become one in the flesh.

Listen carefully, what you are about to hear may shock you. I believe that a man and woman can be married after acknowledging GOD Himself and agreeing to become husband and wife and be married in the sight of GOD and be married without any papers, ring, ceremony, wedding, engagement, or reception. You see, GOD allows us papers for proof to man.

The real ceremony has been long forgotten because of man's heart to lie and cheat because there is no fear of GOD. If there was a real fear of GOD in marriage, there surely would never be divorce. What I see today is fear of man and what he sees and what man thinks and how he perceives, and that encourages selfishness. When you talk about marriage, there should be no other options. Once you have sex with another outside marriage, you bring into that "oneness relationship" another partner connected to that flesh.

That's why GOD tells us to flee fornication because it affects the body like no other sin and sin against themselves. "Do you not know that your bodies are members of Christ? Shall I then take the members of Christ and make them members of harlot? Certainly not! Or do you not know that he who is joined to a harlot is one body with her? For 'the two,' He says, 'shall become one flesh,' but he who is joined to the Lord is one Spirit with Him" (1 Corinthians 6:15–18).

Now who says they shall become one flesh? GOD said, "So now everything about that harlot's body has now become yours. If she has joined herself to thieves, murderers, idolaters, drunkards, all of these are now part of your flesh and only brings uncontrollable desires that you didn't have before."

That's why verse 18: Flee immorality—every sin that a man does is outside the body, but he who commits immorality, sins against his own body. And some wonder why we should wait before having sex. It is because GOD wants purity to take place and His input in the relationship because of obedience. And these desires lead to divorce.

Now I don't want to make it sound like you are doomed because you have already been immoral. That's the reason Jesus died. Mary Magdalene was a harlot, and Jesus cast out seven devils from her, which were evil spirits. Just a note, when evil spirits have access to someone, those spirits have access to their children also. That's why some have children, and though the parents never did drugs or ever had been sexually immoral after they raise that child, that child starts to do things that they didn't do.

A GODLY marriage was never meant to divorce. Never. GOD meant once married, always married. For years I wondered why would a man of GOD, like Moses, command that once a woman has been unfaithful to her spouse, the man decides that he doesn't want her anymore because of her unfaithfulness. After many years of curiosity, GOD finally gave me the answer. It is because GOD's marriages never divorce unless one's spouse dies. If the man's hard heart refuses to stay with her, Moses commanded to take her and stone her to death. After death, the man has the right to marry again. But the death of Christ brings us back to GOD and gives every man the light of life, even the adultness ones. GOD Himself never initiated divorce, but humanistically, He allowed it.

How can GOD initiate divorce and turn around and say, "I hate divorce" (Malachi 2:16)? That would put GOD as dispersing confusion. Because as far as truth is concerned, man would ask, "Which one is it GOD, stay married or divorce?" He keeps it as what He would prefer and His original intention. What GOD wants is never confusing in all His wants and intensions. Operating with wisdom, no man can ever say that God gave a command and then turned around and commanded them to do the exact opposite. Because GOD is not the author of confusion, as in all churches of saints. "So divorce was never commanded by GOD Himself" (1 Corinthians 14:33).

There were men of religious leadership back in the days Jesus walked this earth called the Pharisees. They wanted to test GOD, so they asked Jesus a question. "Is it lawful for a man to divorce his wife for just any reason?" (Matthew 19:3).

Now the first thing that came out of GOD's mouth is the truth and answer. "And he said unto them, 'Have ye not read that he who made them in the beginning made them "male and female," for this reason, a man shall leave his father and mother and be joined to his wife, and the two shall become one flesh?'"(verse 4). Therefore, what GOD has joined together, let no man separate. When he says "no man," he means brother, sister, mother, father, uncle, cousin, friend, or any other. So; it give them this right to ask why then would a man of GOD command to give a certificate of divorce and put her away? Notice what Jesus says in verse 8 that determines if GOD is your Father. He said unto them, "Moses, because of the hardness of your hearts, permitted you to divorce your wives, but from the beginning, it wasn't so." Hardness of heart means that there is another god involved, the god of self. If GOD were your Father, you would maintain your marriage for life, talking to believers, those who truly love GOD.

DIVORCE

Some people get to the point where trouble enters a marriage, and because of past knowledge that divorce is available, it is contemplated and gives place to option. There is only one biblical place in Scripture where if a believer has married an unbeliever and the unbeliever decides to end the marriage (1 Corinthians 7:15). As the Scripture says, this would hold the believer in bondage to the unbeliever seeking to sustain the marriage. But when two believers are married, both have a covenant with GOD from their marriage vows, then the one that seeks divorce is sinning against GOD, and even if one has divorced in GOD's covenant—and I emphasize that in GOD's covenant—they are to remain unmarried to be reconciled back together (1 Corinthians 7:11). If one or both wanted to have hard hearts, this is where Moses gave command to divorce, but it was never GOD Himself.

Over the years, we heard that most people say that Jesus gave the right to divorce and commanded to flee marriage when adultery arises, but that is not the point that Jesus was trying to make. Let me take you to GOD's word and explain what Jesus was saying. The Pharisees came to Jesus like they always do, trying to trick him into saying something they believe is against GOD on the old prophets, and they asked Him, "Is it in the law to have right that a man can divorce his wife for any cause?"

And Jesus said that those that GOD has joined together, let no man put asunder or separate. Now what man was He talking about? He was talking about Moses and the Law of Moses. Now He wasn't going against

Moses but only fulfilling truth because Moses gave command to divorce because he saw hardness of heart where they refuse to let GOD rule their hearts. And when Jesus said that from the beginning, it wasn't so; He meant that GOD never changes His mind and sticks to every covenant He makes until the end. GOD never gave permission to divorce in this verse. Jesus was saying that if two people were married and one decides to divorce and break his/her marriage vows on purpose through another partner, this will cause the other to break their vows with GOD though they may have wanted to keep their vows until death. They were forced to break their vows through another partner themselves because they themselves vowed to GOD to never have another partner. "And I say unto you, whoever shall put away his wife, except it be for fornication, and shall marry another, committeth adultery" (Matthew 19:9).

Here Jesus says (except it be for fornication) this simply means that if a woman has committed fornication against her husband and he divorces her, he can't cause her to commit adultery, because she already has. The point that Jesus was trying to make was that GOD Himself is not in divorce. Watch what it says in the latter end of this verse, "And whoever marries her that is put away from her husband doth commit adultery" (verse 9).

Why does another man commit adultery when he marries a divorced woman? After all, she is divorced. It's because GOD knows human mistakes and expects them to reconcile and come to grips to their covenant.

If you ask your English teacher to explain something, she/he will always take you back to the title and what was the precept of the chapter. The precept from GOD was that divorce was never given by GOD Himself from the beginning of the first marriage of Adam and Eve. The question that was asked was, can a man divorce his wife for anything? And all Jesus did was take us back to GOD's original intention: remain married.

The ones who honor GOD's commands in covenant makes GOD their Father. Once you make a vow to a Godly covenant of marriage, it becomes a law and can only be broken by death. Watch what Jesus says about the law of marriage in GOD's sight. "It is easier for heaven and earth to pass, than one tittle of the law to fail." (Luke 16:17).

Watch what he says right after that: "Whosoever putteth away his wife and marrieth another, committeth adultery; and whosoever marrieth her that is put away from her husband committeth adultery" (verse 18).

Jesus is saying that if you divorce, you commit adultery against the law of GOD. If you marry someone who is divorced, you commit adultery and break GOD's law. A divorced woman/man who says that GOD is their Father cannot remarry. GOD can bring that marriage back to love through forgiveness and faith in GOD. "But if she departs, let her remain unmarried to be reconciled to her husband" (1 Corinthians 7:11).

Through the faith of believers, the husband and wife are to be brought back together. But if one refuses to remarry is an unbelieving person in GOD's sight and the other spouse is not obligated to seek remarriage for the sake of peace (1 Corinthians 7:15).

IF GOD WERE YOUR FATHER

If GOD were your father, you would love Jesus and all His children because you would be expressing the DNA of GOD Himself. Because sons and daughters do what their father do and looks like their father does, carrying his DNA of the Holy Spirit.

Many people talk about GOD because, according to GOD Himself, they already know that there is a GOD in control of this earth, and He can be clearly seen from His creation. He is revealed through our actions. He is revealed through the sun, the moon, and even childbirth. And when we do wrong, the GOD of heaven reveals to us through judgments that we were wrong. "For GOD's Holy wrath and indignations are revealed from heaven against all ungodliness and unrighteousness of men who in their wickedness, suppress and hinder the truth and make it inoperative" (Romans 1:18–20, AMP).

Does that sound like men who function in a way in society that keep the truth about GOD and His functions from operating in people? These are men who don't belong to GOD. Because they push the truth away from themselves and others, follow their ways away from GOD. "For that which is known about GOD is evident to them and made plain in their inner consciousness, because GOD, Himself, has shown it to them" (verse 19). Ever since the creation of the world, His invisible nature and attributes, that is His external power and divinity, have been made intelligible and clearly discernable in and through the things that have been made (His handiworks).

Men are without excuse altogether. They see GOD in creation but don't accept Him as GOD. They train themselves from a human intellect. Seeing GOD in creation comes naturally for all men, but there is a spiritual side of GOD that not all men see, only those who submit to GOD through creation and His son, Christ Jesus.

Through Christ Jesus, GOD gives His Spirit, which carries everything about GOD, even His eternal powers. And GOD's Spirit rests within them and teaches them that GOD is, in fact, true and helps them to overcome the evils of this world.

There has to be a submission to Him in order to be taught. Jesus Himself sent GOD's Spirit back to earth after going back to heaven, when He finished His mission. Jesus spoke to His disciples and gave them comfort because He understood that some of the things that He knew He couldn't tell them because of their human nature. He said, "Howbeit when he, the Spirit of truth, is come, He will guide you into all truth: for He shall not speak of himself; but whatsoever He shall hear, that shall He speak: and He will show you things to come" (John 16:13). It says that whatsoever He shall hear that shall He speak. Who is He hearing from? He is hearing from GOD the Father, and receiving instructions from Him. This opens our minds to the understanding of the Father's authority. Through the scriptures, we find that GOD is bigger than even creation on men, who seem to be wise.

The Bible gives us a deeper understanding of GOD's wisdom. "The foolishness of GOD is wiser than men; and the weakness of GOD is stronger than men" (1 Corinthians 1:25). This is telling me that if GOD was to do something foolish, that foolishness would be smarter than any man; and if GOD had a weakness, that weakness would be stronger than any man.

I don't know about you, but that tells me that if I listen and do the things that GOD says in obedience to him, I would be making a decision that is smarter and stronger than any man. The Father would be pleased with you. It's all about Him you know, and He has ways to help you acknowledge Him. Yes, He helps even our weaknesses and at times speak directly to you, especially when it comes to Christ Jesus, because He is the only one that carries the Father's acceptance. If you get close to His Son, miraculous things will happen apart from many people. "After six days, Jesus taketh Peter, James and John, His brother and bringeth them up onto a high mountain apart and was transfigured before them. And his face did shine as the sun and his raiment was white as the light [signifying a move of GOD] and behold, there appeared unto them Moses and Elias talking with him [Jesus]. Then answered Peter and said to Jesus, Lord it is good for us to be here; if thou will let us make here three tabernacles; one for thee, one for Moses and one for Elias. While He yet spoke, behold, a bright cloud overshadowed them; and behold, a voice out of the cloud which said, 'This is my beloved son, in whom I am well pleased, hear ye him'" (Matthew 17:1–5).

There is a reason why the Father said that He was well pleased with Jesus; because the Father is and should be worthy to be with His Son. God will draw you to Jesus but will not force you to accept Him. GOD leaves that all up to you to make a conscience decision before GOD the Father Himself. Who else is there other than GOD?

Let me take you to a story that GOD gave as an example for us not to follow, where there was a rejection of GOD and His way that brought on a foul spirit. Yes, in obedience to GOD the Father, love for the Father and brother must be considered in order to please GOD.

We all know the story in the Bible about Adam and Eve. Adam and Eve had two sons, Cain and Abel. Some say that they were twins because there was no time in between these two brothers, as we know. These two brothers had different chores. "Now Abel was a keeper of sheep, but Cain was a tiller of the ground. And in process of time, it came to pass that Cain brought some of the fruits of the ground as an offering to the Lord. And Abel also brought of the firstborn of his flock and of the fat portions. And the Lord had respect and regard for Abel and for his offering, but for Cain and his offering, he had no respect or regard. So, Cain was exceedingly angry and indignant, and he looked sad and depressed [foul spirit]; and the Lord said to Cain, 'Why are you angry? And why do you look sad and depressed and dejected? If you do well, will you not be accepted? And if you do not do well, sin crouches at your door; [Now watch how GOD explains to him that by not making the right decision, he rejects GOD's spirit and another spirit will overpower him.] Its desire is for you but you must master it" (Genesis 4:1–7).

What further expresses here is that there are things in this life that wants to master us over the Father, even wicked men that are used by these spirits, and only when we put GOD first is when we find true success; when we don't, it will master us and dominate us. I hear people say all the time, "The devil made me do that." And I say that the devil may have tempted you to do it, but you made the decision to follow through. GOD's word clearly explains to us that by not obeying GOD, we are obeying other voices, whether it be the world, ourselves, or the devil.

I would like to take you to where the GOD of righteous acts allow them to make their own decisions in the Bible, just like He does now, and it is clear that no one can blame others for their decisions because, at the end of the day, the Father punishes us for our own decisions. That tells me that I must take control of my own life and the decisions I make. He commanded Adam first, saying that every tree of the garden can be eaten freely, except for the tree of knowledge of good and evil: "You shall not eat of it, for in the day that you eat of that tree, you will surely die." And I'm quite sure that either GOD or Adam passed it on to Eve after He made her.

This is what I want you to understand—why didn't GOD just block them from the tree so that they couldn't get to it? Because of choice. GOD gave them the right to choose Him or not. And after GOD commanded them, they yielded to the voice of Satan and his cleverness. "Now the serpent [devil] was more subtle than any beast of the field which the Lord GOD had made. And He said unto the woman [notice all He did was say, 'No gun to her head'], 'Yea, hath GOD said ye shall not eat of every tree of the garden? And the woman said unto the serpent, 'We may eat of the fruit of the trees of the garden; but of the fruit of the tree which is in the midst of the garden, GOD said ye shall not eat of it, neither shall you touch it, lest ye die'" (Genesis 3:1) Watch how Satan adds his cleverness and rebellion to her for which she should have told Satan to stay behind her and that she was going to obey GOD alone. (Listen) and the serpent said, "For GOD doth know that in the day ye eat thereof, then your eyes shall be opened and ye shall be as Gods knowing good and evil."

Now I say this, never allow Satan to speak over what the Father has spoken. "And the woman saw that the tree was good for food and it was pleasant to the eyes and a tree to be desired to make one wise."

She took of the fruit there of and did eat and gave also to her husband with her, and they did eat" (verse 6). This is when sin entered the human race and contaminated mankind.

But there is good news. There is a second Adam that was tempted at every point just as Adam and Eve, but He sent the Devil on his way. And if you want to make GOD your Father, you must love Him and everything about Him. In the scriptures, Jesus was speaking to the Jews who believed in GOD but, at the same time, calling Abraham their father, but performing *thing*; unlike Abram, the *thing* symbolized that Satan was really their father. Abraham, whom GOD made the father of our faith in GOD. Their character was not like Abraham because Abraham loved all of GOD's children. The reason they couldn't see that fact is through the way they were treating people; they tapped into a spirit that blinded them from truth.

The Bible calls this darkness, and we all know that when you are in the dark, you can't see. Anyone who claims to be a child of God but opposes the teachings of Christ becomes blind to their goings. And the first command of Christ that is in front of all others is love.

BLINDED BY HATE

"He who says he is in the light and hates his brother is in darkness, until now. He who loves his brother, abides in the light and there is no cause of stumbling in him. But he who hates his brother is in darkness and walks in darkness *and does not know where he is going*, because the darkness has blinded his eyes" (John 2:9–1). In other words, in heaven there is no harm done to each other, and when we don't act on earth as in heaven, it shows that we are not in subjection to GOD nor His Son nor His Spirit, who is light, therefore subjecting ourselves to the darkness of the devil.

But when a person desires to believe GOD, he listens to the teachings of Christ and loves Him by doing what the Father commands. Jesus spoke to some followers and explains to them that ignorantly following Satan's desires blinds you. "Why do you not understand my speech? Because you are not able to listen to my words, you are of your Father the Devil and the desires of your Father you want to do" (John 8:43–47).

The word *Father* in the world dictionary means, figuratively speaking, "a thing that is cause or source." The thing that they believed about Jesus was actually Satan himself. Right now, countless lies is being said about Christ and His followers in order to distort a person's view of Him.

When you participate in these evil deeds, you lose your sense of direction from GOD, making Satan your father and not GOD, who commands you to love. The Scripture goes on to say about a person's intentions to obey. "He who is of GOD hears GOD's words; you therefore do not hear, because you are not of GOD" (verse 47).

Then I will tell you that we should be very certain that our actions toward another brother should most certainly be that of heaven and of Christ. Many of us have been taught things brought up in our childhood that were against heaven. Christ Himself goes on to explain that very fact. When you come to Him, you have another calling that He Himself calls you out of, giving you the power of His Spirit to help you. He talks about what you learned growing up, then He gives you the truth. "You have heard that it was said, 'You shall love your neighbor and hate your enemy. But I say unto you, love your enemy, bless those who hate you and pray for those who despitefully use you and persecute you [why?], that you may be children of your Father which is in heaven'" (Matthew 5:43–45).

I believe that there are countless people who have destroyed themselves just by the way they treat people, especially GOD's children. GOD protects His children, especially those that are in obedience to Him and trust Him. Because when you become a child of GOD, the Father takes control of your life.

Here is the deal—when a person begins to trust GOD and have faith in GOD, and someone turns that person's faith away from GOD through some offense, this inflames GOD's anger at that person. "Whoever shall offend one of these little ones which believe in me, it was better for him that a millstone was hung about his neck and that he was drowned in the depths of the sea" (Matthew 18:6).

Now a millstone was a grinding stone used by women, so large that it had to be turned by a donkey. Jesus gives us an illustration of how it would be if a person turns another person from depending on Him. Just think with me here: If someone had that stone around his neck and then tossed into the sea, what chances would it be for that person to stay at the top? Very slim.

GOD IS YOUR FATHER

So then loving your brother or neighbor who depends on Christ and His teachings is vital to one's life. By reading His words, you come to know Jesus, and He will meet you in spirit face-to-face, with you alone, if you are expecting to hear from Him.

There was a woman that met Jesus face-to-face, and He gave her a chance to know that He was, in fact, her Savior through prophetic word.

MEET JESUS

"Then cometh Him to a city of Samaria, which is called Sychar, near to the parcel of ground that Jacob gave to his son Joseph. Jacob's well was there, Jesus therefore being wearied with his journey, sat on the well; and it was about the sixth hour. There cometh a woman of Samaria to draw water; Jesus said unto her, 'Give me to drink,' prompting a conversation with her just like He is doing you. For his disciples were gone away into the city to buy meat. The woman said unto him, 'How is it that thou being a Jew asketh a drink from me, which am a woman of Samaria for the Jews have no dealings with the Samaritans?' Jesus answered and said unto her, 'If thou knewest the gift of GOD and who it is, that saith to thee, give me to drink; thou wouldest have asked of Him and He would have given thee living water'" (John 4:5–10).

Notice that He said "living water," but the water He was talking about was not water that we drink to quench a thirst; He was talking about the water of life (the Holy Spirit). Everyone that accepts Him receives this water that quenches your thirst for the only true GOD. GOD the Father. "The woman said unto him, 'Sir, thou have nothing to draw with and the well is deep; from where then has thou that living water? Art thou greater than out Father Jacob which gave us the well and drank there of himself and his children and his cattle?' Jesus answered and said unto her, 'Whosoever drinketh of this water shall thirst again; but whosoever drinketh of the water that I shall give him shall never thirst; but the water that I shall give him shall be [in him] a well of water springing up into everlasting life.' The woman saithe unto him, 'Sir, give me this water that I thirst not, neither come hither to draw.' Jesus said unto her knowing that her life was searching for satisfaction, 'Go call thy husband and come hither.'

The woman answered and said, 'I have no husband.' Jesus said unto her, 'Thou has well said, I have no husband. For thou have had five husbands and he whom thou now have is not thy husband; in that saith thou truly'" (John 4:11–18).

Don't you love the way Jesus tells us about our sins but does not condemn us and make us want to turn away from Him with a snobbish religious attitude? In other words, when we listen and obey Christ, we are literally drinking life. The life of heaven. "Jesus says unto you; 'verily verily I say unto you, except ye eat the flesh of the son of man and drink his blood, ye have no life in you'" (John 6:53–58).

This doesn't mean that we are literally eating His flesh and drinking His blood. But by faith, it symbolizes that we are taking upon ourselves His sinless body, which makes us right with GOD through Him. If you really love GOD, you would accept this offer and become His child truly. This is written to believers also because in the Bible days, the people who claimed to be GOD's children were misled and were actually away from GOD. "Therefore we must give the more earnest heed to the things we have heard, lest we drift away. For if the word spoken through angels proved steadfast and every transgression and obedience received a just reward, how shall we escape if we neglect so great a salvation, which at first, began to be spoken by the Lord and was confirmed to us by those who heard Him" (Hebrews 2:1–3).

What we have heard of Him is the fact that He suffered much pain. The pain that we were supposed to suffer, and in that pain, there came not one evil word from His mouth or He Himself would have had to have a savior. And He knew that He was suffering for sinful people, so I ask you this, how far would you have gone if you were giving your life up and in much pain for a car thief, a prostitute, a bank robber? Don't you just love the fact that Jesus never gave up and threw in the towel? If He had, He would have never accomplished what He did on the cross just to make GOD your Father again.

THE FATHER

When we talk about the Father, we talk about the Son, who is Christ Jesus, and we also talk about the Holy Spirit, which is the Spirit of the Father. But in the scriptures, there is an authority of the Father, as far as sovereign rule. The Father was the one that sent Jesus to earth, so that of itself shows the Father's authority, even over Jesus.

Let's go to the Bible and pull out the Father Himself and learn the head of what some believers call the Trinity. The Father is sovereign over all earth, and nothing gets by GOD the Father. If a person believes that then that person develops what the Bible calls the fear of GOD. Jesus said in scripture that "if ye believe in GOD, believe also in me" (John 14:1–2), saying, "Don't just drop the Father, just add me to him." Then He goes on to say, "In my Father's house, there are many mansions." (in reference to the Father being over all, even Him).

In order for a person to be saved, they are touched by the Father first and the Father guides them to Jesus. Whenever you see Jesus in action, you see the Father in action and also the Holy Spirit. They never work outside or apart from one another, but yet at times, you can see by the Spirit and, by their word, the personality of each. When the church of Jesus Christ gets to function like the Trinity, you will then see a powerful church, but one day we will.

"Call no man father upon the earth; for one is your Father, which is in heaven" (Matthew 23:9). Now notice what Christ said. He talked about the Father and His sovereign rule. For you to never allow no man over the rule of your Father. And that one is solo, meaning by itself, without Christ and without the Holy Spirit as far as authority is concerned, but yet one mind with Christ and the Spirit as far as authority is concerned. But yet one mind with Christ and the Spirit. And when each one move, it's under the rule and access of the Father. When Jesus walked this earth, there were men that demanded Him to tell them who gave Him authority to do what He was doing. He had been preaching and telling men that He was Christ, the one that GOD sent to earth, but those who were walking in darkness or in opposition to Him could not grasp the fact that He was the one they were waiting for. Jesus proceeded to explain to them that the thing that He does proves who He is. "As I told you and ye believe not; the works that I do in my Father's name, they bear witness of me" (John 10).

Jesus was saying that He operates in the Father's place, and when they see him and what he does, they see also the Father. This is where the human mind cannot grasp that as a believer of Jesus Christ, we also distribute the hand of GOD. If we are tuned to this world's wisdom, you will never be powerful in GOD. You must operate from the mind of the spirit. The Holy Spirit is the mind of GOD. Before you become powerful in Christ, you have to function from only one knowledge, the knowledge of what GOD says you are and what He wants you to do. From what I read, everything about the Father is one, even you. You are not outside of GOD; you are in the Father, and you must believe that.

THE FATHER'S HEART

We may know some things that is on GOD's heart, but not all things. Sometimes He keeps things to Himself but only gives us what we need to know. The Bible says that GOD gave up His Son to save the whole world. In a nutshell, that's GOD's heart. His heart is love—love for not just His children, but the entire world—that's every man. The written word is GOD's heart. The written word and the expression of the works of the cross. Jesus expressed the Father's heart fully. That is one reason He was so pleased with Him, because whenever a person had faith in GOD for something, if Jesus was near, GOD was able to deliver.

The Bible states that Jesus was tempted at all points even as we are (Hebrews 4:15), which tells me that there were times when Jesus didn't want to bless someone. Here is the spirit of grace that needs to be in operation in every believer. Even though He was tempted to not do it, He did it anyway, in subjection to the Father. The only man that has been tempted in all things but yet never yielded. Can you say that? I know by the scriptures that you can't. Neither can I.

At some point at a young age in life, we knew what was sin and we chose to do it anyway. This is where our soul was contaminated, by doing something that we consciously knew was wrong. And the more we submitted to sin and rejected what our conscience was saying, the quieter the voice of our conscience got until we no longer could hear it. Through Jesus Christ and your confession to Him of your sins, the voice came back clearer. The light of the Father's heart is you; this is why the Father redeems you back to His voice.

Some people display the Father as one who goes around standing over us ready to throw a bolt of lightning, but GOD the Father is a good GOD. The will of the Father is for you to be whole in every area in your life. And your protection comes with Christ Jesus by you becoming one in spirit. The Father, the Son, and the Holy Spirit is always in agreement. There is no substance on earth that does not carry some presence of the Spirit. There is no man on earth that can insanely say that GOD doesn't see Him. The Father's presence is everywhere, but there is a special presence of the Father that we carry through obedience as children of GOD. The more you yourself individually seek to obey GOD, the more presence you have with you. It's called the anointing. "He that dwelleth in the secret place of the Most High shall abide under the shadow of the Almighty" (Psalm 91:1).

Anytime you see someone's shadow, you know for a fact that person is right there by you, and there is a reason he is right there, by your own choice. "I will say of the Lord, He is my refuge and my fortress: My GOD, in Him will I trust" (verse 2). It is because by faith, you trust Him. Your faith in the Father is displayed through your actions. By you acting out what He says, His power surrounds you or takes the atmosphere. "Surely, He shall deliver thee from the snare of the fowler, and from the noisome pestilence" (verse 3).

Every word that you are reading right now is for you because your heart is in the Father's plan. Everything that goes on in this life is in the works for all the Father's people. We just need to learn how to let GOD do His work upon this earth (just like His Son). When you read your Bible and study the life of Christ in a revealed text (Matthew, Mark, Luke, John), you find Jesus, who is the apple of GOD's eye, allowed the Father, even when He was in pain.

I know that sometimes we don't fully grasp the fact that we are His children, but at the same time, He allows us to suffer tribulations in this world; but we need to think about other people just as Christ thought about us. Those other people need your participation in Christ Jesus. In other words, you are on your cross for people who mistake you. And when you do that, you yourself is an expression of the Father's heart. In His heart, He doesn't put Himself first; He put us first. And if he put us first, then we must return the favor and put others first. This is how we fill heaven.

The Bible states that "he who wins souls is wise" (Proverbs 11:30). We are not really wise until we direct people to Christ. When we direct people to Him, we are in subjection to the Holy Spirit, who has all the knowledge of GOD, and this same knowledge is in you and is flowing out from you and to you, giving you the knowledge of Christ through whatever level you submit to Him. By the Spirit of GOD constantly flowing through you, it gives you an understanding and reveals truth. Jesus says that "if you continue in my word, you shall know the truth and the truth shall make you free" (John 8:32). He is talking about you becoming a part of GOD's heart by purification of spirit. Through your obedience to GOD's word, the Holy Spirit transforms your thoughts, plans, and goings into the Father's heart. GOD never changes and He is always who He is and always was. He doesn't submit to our goings, but we submit to His. Once you know the truth, you can now identify a lie when it comes and is now able to make wise decisions. In other words, you become GOD Himself. Not that you are GOD, but that you function from His heart.

Do you know what kind of privilege that is, for the creator of this earth to give you the opportunity to distribute Him. Glory to GOD. Your heart has to get to the point where you have to step out by faith. Study the scriptures and study the heart of GOD, and then knowing that He is with you, make a move and deliver. Sometimes you don't have to ask the person who is in need, but just if you see the need, then you allow GOD to move through you. If you don't or if you see that need and don't give to that person, then you cannot have GOD's heart dwelling in you. You see, just like everything else, His heart has to be cultivated. You are working toward becoming pure toward Him. There has to be points where you don't feel like giving, and that is the point where the spirit cannot drive out that part of human thinking on, believe it or not, filthiness of flesh. Yes, it's you that doesn't want to give, but GOD is always willing. The problem that some believers have is that there are times that we pray for people, but there are times when prayer is not sufficient for that moment, only simply giving. When you have what that person needs in your possession and have enough to give them and you don't, you sin against the Father's heart.

What if you knew a sick person or a person that hadn't eaten in three days, and you give someone the food to take to that person but they don't give it? How would you feel? That answers the question that many people have that when we look around this earth and see hunger and plenty of other needs, and we ask, "Where is GOD?" Well, through greed and selfishness, humanity rejects to distribute His heart. Yes, the Father gives every man the privilege to do so through human dominion, which was given to Adam. This, my friend, is one of the most important assets and privileges that the Father gives. Because it proves us. I prove whether we belong to the Father or Satan.

I'm going to take you through a few verses to explain what I mean. Keep in mind that the heart of the Father is to submit to His kind of unselfish love. The love that tells you that you are a child of GOD. You can know by your own submission if you belong to heaven. A continuous submission cultivates your knowing and gives you a release from fear. "We know that we have passed from death to life because we love the brethren" (1 John 3:14). Now look at those first two words, "*We know.*" This tells me that my knowing comes from how I distribute my love to the brethren. By submitting to the fruit of the spirit, who carries this knowledge, I know. It goes on to say that "he that loveth not his brother abideth in death."

The word *abideth* is translated to "remain." So why does he remain in death? Because of the spirit that he submits to. GOD's spirit is life. When a person rejects to move by the heart of GOD, he/she rejects life, thus remains in death. Because that person sees the need but refuses, the Father, not man, considers that hate and murder.

The next verse continues from that verse: "Whosoever hateth his brother is a murderer. Ye know, that no murderer hath eternal life abiding in him" (verse 15).

By you not operating by the fruit of the Father's spirit is a spirit of murder. You are literally killing that person as far as love is concerned, and you are showing that you don't really appreciate the fact that Christ laid down His life to save you and give you life; that becomes an outright dishonor to Christ and a yielding to His works and your chance to become like Him, in which should be your ultimate drive. With a drive of the spirit to become like Christ, this is how we come to know GOD's love: "Hereby perceive we the love of GOD, because he laid down his life for us: we ought to lay down our lives for the brethren" (verse 16).

Keep in mind that these words are talking about a conscience decision. It's not something you get just because you talk good about someone—that has its place in prayer—but remember, I said that there are times to just give. By you leaving the scene of that need and you don't have compassion and give, you reject the Father's heart. "But whoso hath this world's good, and seeth his brother in need, and shutteth up his bowels of compassion from him, how dwelleth the love of GOD in him" (verse 17).

The scriptures says, "He shutteth up his bowels of compassion," which means that compassion he wants to give is there, but that person made a conscience decision not to help, thus rejecting what GOD wanted to do. It means the GOD's love cannot dwell in that person by choice, thus rejecting the Father's heart.

So now we see that we must come to a conclusion that we must honor the Father and love Him because He loved you first.

TRUE GRACE

Everything that GOD gives through Jesus Christ is grace first. The word *grace* means "special favor or privilege." When Jesus died for us, it was a special privilege. When Jesus died for us, it was a special favor. A favor that we didn't deserve. It was a favor that GOD gave while knowing every sin that you and I will ever commit. Can you imagine a person robbing a bank while you are watching and then when he exits the door and comes into your presence, you start to give that person special favor knowing what he has done? That's what GOD does. Can you imagine a person having a wife and loving another woman behind her back then you knowing this and you give him special favor and treating him with kindness even though he has committed adultery? That's the way GOD treats us all.

Now you know why the Bible states that natural man/mind cannot receive the things of GOD. This grace of the cross to an extent can only be distributed by the spirit of GOD. Let me ask you a question, do you think that GOD was watching those two guys before they committed those sins? Yes, He was. He was standing over each one of them and was with them every step. Not saying that GOD let us get away with sin because He is a "just" GOD and a GOD of divine understanding; here is why: If GOD were to pay each of us for the things we do wrong, none of us would be alive today. But because His divine plan wants every human to escape the gates of hell and make heaven. He overlooks sin, giving each of us favor we don't deserve, hoping we realize our mistakes and turn from our mistakes and accept Jesus. If you call yourself a child of GOD, depending on how much you believe GOD is how you will distribute grace. When a normal person sees you sin, their favor turns from you and may never come back, and every time they see you, that sin becomes fresh to their minds. That's the natural mind. We need to come to grips of how good GOD is. That's the reason He gives grace for you to know Him because favor, unlike the natural man, captures your attention because when we know that someone knows that we have done wrong, we kind of expect their judgment. We expect their harsh words; we expect their bad treatment, but when we find favor on the other side of sin, it captures our hearts because it's not natural. GOD wants you to know that He loves each of us.

The grace of GOD is not displayed like it should be through the believer, where we are mistreated, but still deliver goodness. Most Christians hold even their own brothers in bondage. They deal with you in a way not by the Holy Spirit; they deal with you in a way that keeps you condemned, which is a selfish human spirit. In order for conviction to arise in the one that is sinning, the love of GOD must be present, assisting a displeasure of sin. That is who GOD is; that is who Jesus is, but some Christians, when they see a person fall in sin, they seek to tear that person down and seek to destroy everything that person tries to do, which is never generated from the spirit of GOD, but is much more like the destroyer/Satan, the accuser. This type of action keeps a person condemned and in bondage to man and the fear of man. This type of action keeps a person's actions trying to please man and not GOD because, after all, the way they treat a sinner directs that sinner's attention to man and not GOD.

"Christ has set us free" (Galatians 5:1, NLV). Now make sure that you stay free and don't get tied up again in the slavery of the law. Ungracious acts keep a person seeking to please man and GOD through the law, which is just religion. So ungracious acts toward a sinning brother turns a person into a religious hypocrite because of disfunction of the Holy Spirit. The human agenda keeps a person's focus on the law, but when a person delivers grace or the Holy Spirit, it keeps that person focused on GOD's heart and gives him a knowing that all he needs is GOD. "If you are trying to make yourself right with GOD by keeping the law, you have been cut off from Christ! You have fallen away from GOD's grace" (verse 4, NLV).

Religion justifies you by the law, because in their eyes, you cannot make one mistake, ever. (This is not justifying sin, but opens the door for the Holy Spirit to work on a person's heart.) If GOD commands us to love each other, and we don't, it is impossible for you to say that your faith toward another is working because your faith has to be in GOD, which is in tune with His command, which is in tune with His son who delivers grace. "What is important is our faith which is only expressed through love, as the King James say [faith that worketh by love], so their actions are doing a sinning broth no good" (verse 6, NLV).

FOCUS ON THE SPIRIT

What do you think happens if we allow the Holy Spirit His full authority? He will give a person a divine understanding first, because there has to be an understanding before repentance, because if a person doesn't understand what they are doing, then why should he repent? Everything is done by GOD's spirit, not ours. That's how grace works.

Grace helps us to trust GOD and believe in His Son, and if you believe in His Son, who delivers grace, then—and only then—can you say that GOD is your Father. But one must not think that just because GOD is so gracious, we can just take advantage of His spirit and the Son of GOD and just do whatever we want because GOD is so good.

No. GOD is not good to us so that we can become fools and neglect His goodness. That's called taking GOD's grace and turning it into lasciviousness, which means that a person is now operating by a more lustful spirit and is denying Christ Himself and puts him in a spirit against GOD, which brings judgment. The same way that GOD treated us, we should deliver back to Him. Let me teach you how GOD first got my attention. First of all, I knew that there was grace upon my life because of the sinner that I once was, but I had a mother who was saved, and she talked to me and my brothers from time to time, even though we were in the street partying and spinning records. My attention stayed on that one fact that GOD was good to me, and this got my attention and started to soften my heart to the point where I began tossing back and forth in my decisions whether to remain in the world or come to Christ.

One night, I was in my room, and something prompted me to get up and go get my mother's family bible, so I did. I opened it up, and for some strange reason, it opened to one verse that seemed to be what I needed at that very time. I now know that the spirit of GOD hit me with divine understanding, and I decided to give in to GOD. Here is where it gets to where GOD touched my heart to the point where I can never deny the fact that GOD is real and how the Holy Spirit quickens us. After I decided to give in to GOD, I closed the Bible and stood up and proceeded to take the Bible back into the living room. When I took my first step, holding the Bible with both hands, it automatically went up, me still holding it; it went up and softly pet the top of my head twice. When I took that next step, chills filled my whole body, because I realized that I had nothing to do with that Bible tapping me on the head.

From that day forth, I was never the same, and GOD has been alive in my heart from that day. My mom delivered grace for years and changed my life. By grace, GOD let me know that I was on the right track, and, my brother, you are no different than I. The Bible states in John 5:9, "We receive the witness of man, but the witness of GOD is greater." That means that when the spirit of GOD Himself touches your heart, He leaves a greater influence of GOD, which will never leave you. He leaves the kind of influence that if you sin, you do it knowing that you are wrong, because if you are convicted, then the Holy Spirit has a place there in your heart. GOD wants a direct relationship with all of us, but a direct relationship gives you more power and a direct attention to GOD and accountability to GOD alone.

Now grace empties you of the burden of trying to please GOD through works, because the Bible states that in order to fully please GOD, you have to completely. Does that sound like somebody to you? Yes, Jesus. This is how He pleased GOD, because He knew that it would be impossible for us to please GOD this way. This means that He has a sinless body, and when you give your life to him, GOD considers you a part of His Son and cleanses your past from every sin that you ever committed. Your continuous faith in Christ, sustaining the spirit of grace that delivers grace and extends it to this world.

The whole law of GOD is summed up in the fact that we deliver to others what GOD has delivered to us. A person that is trying to please GOD through the law is under a curse or bondage. But the law that we give by the spirit frees a person from a curse on bondage. There was a man that asked Jesus to show them the Father/ GOD, and Jesus spoke to him and said that if you have seen me, you have seen the Father. In other words, He was saying that all the free things that I give is GOD Himself. Do you deliver grace, or does a person have to perform for you? One thing I've learned is when you have to perform for people to receive from them, you can feel that bondage. You can feel that spirit of control that wears you down.

GOD wants His children to be free and joyful. The GOD that I serve is gracious.

Any person who puts people in bondage is from Satan himself. There was a woman that Satan had kept bound with sickness for many years, and the religious leaders were so focused on the law that they wanted Jesus to obey their law of the Sabbath, which keeps a person in bondage to man and never can receive healing. If Jesus would have listened to them, He could not be gracious, so He didn't and told them this: "You hypocrite. [Meaning that they say that they are of GOD, but don't deliver GOD. And He goes on to deliver grace and says] Does not each of you, on the sabbath, loose his ox or his ass from the stall and lead him away to watering? Ought not this woman, being a daughter of Abraham, whom Satan hath bound these eighteen years be loosed from this bond on the sabbath day?" (Luke 13:15–17).

Here Jesus implied that grace should be delivered anytime it is needed. There should not be a special day. GOD is a giver, and in reality, they didn't know GOD. If we don't give grace the way GOD does, we don't know GOD. Your level of grace expresses your level of how much you know

GOD. We should live by faith in the Son of GOD, and if our faith is in Him, then we are gracious even under pressure. Because that pressure will reveal if GOD is your Father.

JESUS CHRIST THE SON

There is no higher authority than that of Jesus, and as he reigns, so do we in this life—that is, if we are submitted to Him. (The word *reign* means to "have sovereign power".) One thing you must know is that suffering with Jesus gives you authority and power to reign with Him.

First, let me fill you in on what suffering with Him means GOD gave us a command to not take vengeance ourselves and to let Him take vengeance and while you submit to His command, your old man wants to take vengeance. But by your submission, you don't allow Him, so your suffering is in your flesh who wants to pay back everyone who treats you wrong.

But now you are a new creature, and your old man is dying and you are operating from your spirit man who is receiving power from the Holy Spirit to maintain strength. Therefore, you are in with the same sufferings of your Master, Jesus, and have become under the same authority. Under the authority of GOD's spirit, when you speak, there's favor from GOD, because you are in line with Him and His Spirit. But when you don't submit, you have human power, but not GOD's. Mountains move when you speak and act under GOD's spirit. When Jesus spoke to the wind, it obeyed. He spoke to the sea, and it became still. He spoke to a bush, and that bush withered away right before His disciples' eyes. Now that is power operating in His name. *In the Royal law (love) there is suffering like the Master because we are commanded to love, even when treated wrong. Because you are no longer working from your flesh and are now working from your spirit, who is in communion with the Holy Spirit.* It is no longer you whom they are doing wrong; it's GOD now. When they say something about your actions, it's GOD they are blaspheming, and that becomes a danger for them.

In the days of Moses, he was under the rule of GOD when he was leading them out of bondage. Some of the children murmured at what he was commanding them to do from GOD. Moses wanted to set the record straight. Watch what he said to these men. "The Lord heareth your murmurings which you murmur against Him: and what are we? Your murmurings are not against us, but against the Lord" (Exodus 16:8).

If GOD was to allow this type of thing to go on, it would sweep through many people and turn many away from the commands of GOD. That tells me that my safety is not in people but in the commands of GOD. The only way safety in people is involved is when it's tied to listening to GOD. Loyalty to His commands comes first.

THE MIND OF CHRIST

In the mind of Christ, His love moved Him for the entire world, and if we are to have the mind of Christ, the "we" in our hearts is for every human being. If you say that you love GOD, then your mind must be like His. There is only one way to put your mind like His— by accepting His way, His messages, and His love.

You can have different kinds of love: there is human love and there is GOD's love. Human love, the Bible talks about how our parents loved us and chastened us as children, but GOD explains that it is selfish love (Hebrews 12:9–10). They truly loved us, yes, but GOD loves us more than our parents, and GOD's chastening is different than our parents.

The mind of Christ is always connected to His love, so in GOD's love, He loves in spite of anything we do. The spirit of GOD gives us the mind of Christ. It is impossible to have the mind of Christ without His spirit, so if you are not saved, then you cannot have the mind of Christ. You may have a zeal of His mind, but not His mind because His spirit is His mind by Him knowing the deep things of GOD.

The Holy Spirit helps us to understand GOD. He helps us to understand Himself. He helps us to understand Jesus Christ, and He helps you to understand yourself. With His spirit, we can function just like Jesus. Inside His mind, Jesus tells us to "only believe." That means to not meditate on the negative but on the fact that what you are believing for is completed. Everything else is cast down because if you give place to it, then it has a place in your mind. "Only believe"—that's the mind of Christ. The Father, the Son, and the Holy Spirit has one mind, and it is always the same all the time. The only thing that is on GOD's mind is healing. The only thing that is on GOD's mind is prosperity. GOD is not like humans. He never once made not one person sick and never once made one man poor or destroyed his finances.

In my own life, I found that man is just back and forth in their minds. One day they love you and the next month they hate you. One day they want to be with you and the next day they don't. That is not how the mind of Christ functions. His mind is always in a forward movement.

Jesus said this (understand His mind): "If so you will always have the power of GOD." It is comforting to know that no matter what comes up in my life, I can come to Jesus for help, even when I have sinned, because it is Him you come to for forgiveness, and there is nowhere else. Always know this: one thing is that GOD loves you and He is always for you. "Which things also we speak, not in words which man's wisdom teaches, but which the Holy Ghost teaches" (1 Corinthians 2:13).

That tells me that man has a wisdom and also the Holy Spirit has a wisdom. Now here is the power. The one spoken under the authority of man carries the power of man. The one spoken under the authority of Jesus Christ carries the power of GOD. The wisdom spoken under the authority of Christ adds life. The mind of Christ is life only and has nothing to do with death or darkness.

It is impossible for you to be in GOD when you are harming another's life or doing any kind of evil against another person, because His mind is for life only. GOD will never insult any man. Correction, only, but not insults. GOD convicts, but not condemns. There is a natural man in all of us, and there is a spiritual man.

It is up to you who you speak from, and who you speak from is who you glorify, whether yourself or GOD. Your natural man does not accept the things of GOD and cannot know them (verse 14), because it takes

GOD's spirit to accept and know what GOD wants. If Christ is not your Savior, I'm sorry, but you don't have the mind of Christ, which is GOD's (verse 16). Who has known the mind of Christ that he may instruct him? We "believers" have the mind of Christ. With the mind of Christ, I'm able to tell sin, "Nope, not today and not tomorrow either." You don't think that Jesus was tempted to curse someone with His mouth? Yes, He was. He was tempted at every point, so that power of the Holy Spirit is to sustain you from hurting other people (use it).

And you have to know that it is an on-purpose thing. Submit to His mind on purpose. You have to exercise your thoughts to know good from evil. Of course, you make many mistakes, but submit to His mind and allow only GOD to function through you and your mind. In the mind of Christ, He wants every person upon this earth to have what He has. (Every person, that is why He died to bring us to heaven with Him and GOD.) Then your actions and words should be that of grace. Jesus loves you just like He loves Himself. We should love our neighbors just like we love ourselves. If you are wealthy, then you should want your neighbor to be wealthy. You are loving him just like you love yourself. When you see how Christ acts, you will know GOD. Humanity wants to tear you down to fix you, but not GOD.

In the wisdom of GOD, tearing someone down does harm to them and your relationship with them. But a fool will destroy their own relationship through the wisdom of man. When Jesus dealt with people, you can feel His rebuke and you also feel His love through the spirit of GOD. Trust me, there is a difference. That door to Christ's heart is always open. If your mind is in tune with His mind, you can have perfect peace.

I ask you that if you don't have peace, seek to have the mind of Christ, forgive these that have done you wrong and bless them instead, giving honor and glory to Jesus and watch the spirit of GOD bring a rest to your soul. If the spirit of GOD is the leader in your life, who can make Him/you worry; who can make Him/you fearful? If you are led by GOD's spirit, then you, my friend, belong to GOD. If you are led by the spirit, then you have the mind of Christ. "Whosoever transgresseth and abideth (remains) not in the doctrine of Christ, does not have GOD" (2 John 9).

The word *transgresseth* means to go beyond limits or to violate commands (sinning). We have to remain in what He says at all times. It is not an option, it's a fact. If you seek to obey His commands, then you have GOD "He that abideth [remains] in the doctrine of Christ have both the Father and the Son" (verse 9). Reaching the Father is obeying His son. "Let us therefore, as many as be perfect, be thus minded; and if anything, be otherwise minded. GOD shall reveal even this unto you. Nevertheless, whereto we have already attained [arrived], let us walk the same rule, let us mind the same thing" (Philippians 3:15–16). Any person who walks other than what Christ commands is an enemy of the cross. They are enemies of the mind of Christ whose end is destruction as it says (verse 19). Outside of the mind of Christ is destruction. Inside of the mind of Christ, there is life, everlasting life. When you express your actions toward others, you are proving to GOD whom you serve, whether Him, yourself, man, or the devil. GOD gives you that freedom because how else will GOD know who you serve, if he didn't let you express yourself? All at the same time, GOD will let you know what is right and allow you to act.

Never exalt man. Always exalt the Father and the Son. In the Bible, how do you see Christ function when they caught the woman in adultery and they wanted to stone her to death, but let her go and told her to go and sin no more? Christ is asking you, "How did you see me function, when Peter denied me three times? Did I condemn him? No. How did you see me function when Judas turned his back on me and stole money from the money bag? How did you see me treat him and I knew all along that he was going to betray me? Did you see me act ugly with him because I knew? No."

Now you see His mind is to allow GOD's love to penetrate the hearts of evil men. Some will receive His love and do better, but some will not. We must hold ourselves accountable to GOD on our own even though we receive strength from the brotherhood. When you allow GOD to work through you, you are allowing His power, His might, His ability. Therefore, it is GOD Himself. That is what it means to die to self; you don't allow what your mind wants, but what His mind wants. If someone wants you to submit to their authority and they are not leading you to function like Christ, then you have the right not to submit. GOD will never send an authority that is leading you away from His Son.

The only thing that will be left with you the day you stand before the Son of GOD on judgment day will be how you listened to His voice.

HIS VOICE

Even though you just read this part about Jesus Christ, you can hear His voice telling you how He acts, in a way to keep your listener as being precious and important. I don't know if you have ever worked in American stores, but in American stores, the owners always keep their employees in a mindset that the customer is always right. Therefore, in the heart of the customer, he/she feels important and is not disrespected; therefore, the customer feels welcome at all times, and when they feel welcomed, the first store they think of when they need something that the store carries is that store. It is the same with Christ. The reason Christ acts the way He does is because He, in all His wisdom, knows for a fact that He is the only way to the Father. Therefore, He is very cautious of a person's heart as to not turn them to another source of comfort or protection. His love is always the same at all times.

What would you do if you had parents that you felt wouldn't even understand you? Or you know that if you came to them, they would only ridicule you or blame you for what's wrong or just make you feel miserable about the whole thing? They would lose your trust because of their actions. Jesus, in all His works with all His followers, makes you feel very important at all times, and it works for Him, so what about you? It is called grace. Listen to what He told the Father after communing with Him in spirit and giving Himself for His followers just so they can go free.

Judas came with officers to take Jesus, so He asked them who they were looking for, knowing all the time. And the second time He asked, He said this: "Jesus answered, 'I have told you that I am He: if therefore ye seek me, let these go their way: That the saying might be fulfilled which He spoke of them which thou gavest me have I lost none'" (John 18:8–9).

The voice of Christ completely goes against human wisdom on the move of the people; it is only in spirit that we have received and in a love for even our enemies. You see, when you submit to GOD, there is a voice of the spirit that you also receive. A voice that goes along with your own choice, believe it or not, and your intentions of how you treat people. If you intend to treat those you encounter the way Christ commands, then you are in what the Bible calls light, and it is where His voice is. The second you submit to another GOD, the voice of Christ is diminished by choice. "If GOD were your Father, you would love me" (John 8:42). In other words, Jesus was saying to them that if your acts were in line with GOD, you would hear Him say, "Love my son," because they would know for a fact that GOD sent Him, because the voice of GOD is in His commands.

Jesus explains plainly to them the reason they couldn't hear Him in the voice of His speeches. He asks and then explains, "Why do ye not understand my speech? Even because ye <u>cannot</u> hear my word, ye are of your father the devil. [They were hearing the devil's commands, not GOD's.] The lusts of your father ye will do" (verse 43–44). So they were subjected to the voice of Satan in which he recruits many people. Here is the most frightening part: If you study the scriptures, these were law enforcement and religious leadership led by a man who turned against GOD. "They were all led by a voice that was not GOD's" (John 18:3). This, my friend, is the heart of deception. It is who you intend to follow by submission and belief. "And Jesus spoke to those who were of another voice. 'But ye believe not, because ye are not my sheep as I said unto you. My sheep hear my voice'" (John 10:26–27).

Jesus was saying to them that you don't intend to do what He says, so you can't hear Him. So, I ask you, who do you intend to make your Father? If it is GOD, then buckle yourself and submit to His word individually, and this makes GOD your Father.

HOW TO BE SMART IN GOD

If you were to ask this question, who is the smartest person you know, whether men living or have passed, who would it be? Some would say Einstein, some would say their science teacher in college, some would even say Mom or Dad. But who is really the smartest person that ever lived? Well, if you really want to know the truth, let's go to GOD's word and let Him do the explaining. Don't you think that GOD will point out smart people? This is what I want you to know he revealed to me—that those who are attached to human wisdom as the ultimate wisdom, are the ones who GOD Himself brings to shame. Because if people look to the wisdom of men as the ultimate wisdom, then take a guess whose wisdom is being despised? Yes, GOD.

When GOD is despised, He operates in a way to show you how foolish you are because this kind of mindset can destroy any man. GOD's wisdom carries His spirit, and man's wisdom carries the spirit of man. Man's wisdom puffs you up to a deception where a man can get to the point that he has no need of GOD. That's why GOD brings that person to knowing how foolish he really is, sometimes corporately. Their minds are in another spirit, so when Godly wisdom is presented to them, it can't register. "For the preaching of the cross is foolishness to them that perish" (1 Corinthians 1:18). Now why does it sound like foolishness to those that are headed for destruction? That is what the word *perish* means. It means to become destroyed or ruined. Or you can put it like some people say, "Going to hell." It means that person preaching the cross of Christ is giving you a kingdom, where in that kingdom, there are actions of that kingdom, where there is no fighting or retaliation because the person that doesn't retaliate stops Satan in his tracks, so-to-speak.

The Bible states that Jesus came to destroy the works of the devil. "So Satan could not get Jesus to hurt one person in which he identified GOD the Father" (1 John 3:8). If you have been on this earth for a number of years, we know that men retaliate or get you back. When they look at these actions, they sound foolish to love someone that does you wrong. But here is a hint of who the smart man is: He allows GOD Himself to vindicate, not Himself. Because even if that person deserves to be punished, your hands are clean because in every action, there is a reaction in the spirit.

This next verse explains what GOD does to a person who does not acknowledge GOD as superior, but those who revere the Father, knows that the cross is good. "But unto us which are saved it is the power of GOD. For it is written, I, will destroy the wisdom of the wise and bring to *nothing*, the understanding of the prudent."

The way wise men understand is different from the way GOD understands. But even if we don't understand some things GOD commands, if we do things his way, this, my friend, is the smart man. The Father is on your side. What GOD really does through His way is to keep Satan away from you, because the way you respond to people could give him access to you.

Believe it or not, Satan has rights and his rights are what Jesus keeps us from, through GOD's presence of the Spirit of love. "We know that whosoever is born of GOD sinneth not: but he that is begotten of GOD, keepeth himself and the wicked one touches him not" (1 John 5:18). Now let's pull smartness from this verse.

Listen to those two words: Keepeth himself. Keepeth himself. Now we know that there is a part that we play in the matter. It's not just all GOD, but GOD responds to our actions, whether we believe Him or not. So that says that love brings GOD to you, but hate drives GOD away.

To answer that question in your heart, that if GOD is love and doesn't really want to hurt us, then where does the destruction come from? Now you are really about to add smartness to your spirit because the destruction is GOD's judgment, where the Father is always watching over every matter and nothing can get by Him. No love, no hate; He watches everything and doesn't force Himself on you to obey. He wants us to individually choose Him through selfwill, and self-will is the only true obedience. A forced will is not obedience. GOD watches everything you do and decides whether you want more of Him or less of Him.

If you choose to disobey, then GOD has no right to you. Through His judgments, He can't help but to allow you to what you have chosen. If you chose not to believe GOD, then take a guess who you have chosen. Yes, you are right. You have chosen Satan, and his only motive is to steal, kill, and *destroy*. You have given him a right to you. If some person thinks from a human mind and thinks that they are helping someone by hurting them, you, my friend, are being used by Satan. If the Bible states that GOD is love, then only love can come from GOD. If you are in GOD just like Jesus on the cross was in the spirit of His Father, then your hands are *clean from evil*. "This then is the message which we have *heard of Him*, and declare unto you, that GOD is light and *in Him* is no darkness at all" (1 John 1:5). That tells us that GOD's motives are always light/good and not darkness/evil. Yes, it says none at all.

Let's get a better view on light and darkness. In Greek, the word *darkness* means "not knowing GOD." If the cross is light then darkness is everything that is anti-GOD. But GOD rules the darkness. The biblical view of darkness and light offers a unique contrast. There is no thought that darkness is equal in power to GOD's light. The absolute, sovereign GOD rules over the darkness and the powers of evil. GOD knows the darkness and everything it contains. GOD rules over the darkness because He created it. GOD uses the darkness for His own purposes and to bring judgment on evil-doers, evil nations, and false prophets.

It was what He used to judge His son in the place where we should have been judged. GOD allowed darkness. The Son of GOD spoke to those who used darkness and said, "This is your hour and the power of darkness" (Matthews 8:12). Those who operate in darkness are blinded by the darkness. They couldn't recognize the innocence of Christ Jesus because they were rulers of the darkness. The sole leader behind all darkness is, of course, Satan himself, who has no respect for life.

Satan used these leaders for his own purpose. The Bible states that had they known, they would not have crucified the Lord of Glory. First Corinthians 2:8 explains that the authorities of the time of Christ were doing something that they were ignorant of. Satan had them deceived like he does now at times. But Jesus says that the way to recognize His people is that they have the light of life, meaning they respect life, period (smart). It is frightening to see the kind of religious spirit sweeping America that says it belongs to GOD and, in judgment, for GOD.

In GOD's judgments, GOD is absent and Satan is at work, and all who follow the darkness of Satan will be cast into the lake of fire with him. Show me one time in the Scripture where Jesus sought the death of one man. Jesus, who is the image of His Father. Only Satan seeks death because in darkness, GOD the Father has given him that right to do it, and he has every right.

Jesus spoke the fact that GOD was absent. "My GOD, My GOD, why has thou forsaken me?" (Matthew 27:46).

GOD was gone; the Father had left Him all alone to die for the sins of the world, and Satan had a ball and, at the same time, defeated himself by his own actions. If you take actions yourself against people, take a guess whose part you play. If you play his part, then Satan is your father, not GOD. Even though you may feel pleasure in your flesh when you hurt someone, it's not GOD.

The Bible states that there is pleasure in sin for a while (Hebrews 11:25). Just because it feels good, does not mean that it's right. Wisdom is not what you feel; wisdom is just plainly submitting to GOD. GOD is all wise, not us. Earthly wisdom is foolish to GOD. That is why we have to do what He says to become wise or smart.

The Holy Spirit is called the spirit of wisdom because He carries all the knowledge of GOD. Whatever the Father does is smart. Whatever you do in reference to their Father makes you and I smart.

PUTTING YOUR ROOTS DEEP IN GOD

If we don't have our roots deep, they can be easily plucked up. I'm talking about His word, following the Lord Christ and doing the things that He is calling you to do. We should have our roots deep in Him in understanding. I've seen when troubles hit me as a young believer in past times. We stop following GOD. People can tell us certain things, and immediately, we turn from GOD. "Men will no longer endure sound" (2 Timothy 4:1–3) doctrine.

After the word is given by a minister—there are many ministers in this world—some people get home from church, and you ask them what was the message today? They may tell you a few things, but from what they say gives you the impression that they really weren't listening. I believe that type of learning is a waste of time when you don't listen deeply to what is being said. We must meditate on GOD's word longer and don't just throw it to the side and continue on with our day. We can be distracted about many things. If you have deep roots, your fruits are sweeter; your tree grows better, and when the wind blows, your tree will not falter.

Because your roots are deep, you will not turn from the Lord because of nutrition of the Spirit—in His deep understanding. The thing GOD sent Jesus to do explains a lot. "And He came to Nazareth, where he had been brought up and as His custom was, He went into the Synagogue on the Sabbath day and stood up to read" (Luke 4:16) (Jesus found Himself in the word). Watch what it says about His mission. "The spirit of the Lord is upon me, because He hath anointed me to preach the Gospel to the poor. He hath sent me to heal the broken hearted, to preach deliverance to the captives, and recover sight to the blind."

The captives that GOD sent Him to deliver as people who are in bondage to man. In this life where you are in bondage, when you're experiencing the Spirit of GOD, a man is liberated. The Bible says, "Where the Spirit of the Lord is, there is liberty" (Corinthians 3:17), "so a man is liberated." In other words, *set free*. When you are seeking GOD like you should, there is rest for you.

In the next verse, it says, "GOD sent him to tell the blind that they can see again" (verse 18). This is not only just talking about a literal blind person, it's also talking about a person who has eyes that can see but yet are still blind to the things of GOD. Certain things or sins that we do against GOD blinds us from seeing the things of GOD.

Jesus, in His actions, was sent to open our eyes to what we are doing, and this is what GOD wants us to do. Putting our roots deep is when we take action to what the words say. I've seen some of my own friends start to do things for GOD, and the minute they are tested, as soon as something negative happens, the first thing they do is fall right back into the world. "My son, pay attention to what I say. Remember my commands" (Proverb 2:1-5, ESV).

How can we remember the commands of GOD? By meditating on what's been said? Verse 2 says, "Listen to wisdom and do your best to understand. Ask for good judgment. Cry out for understanding." In other words, we need to develop a desire to hear GOD. Watch how the scriptures make the word of GOD as valuable using things that we consider valuable on this earth. "Look for wisdom like silver, search for it like hidden treasure. If you do this, you will understand what it means to respect the Lord, and you will come to know GOD" (verse 4).

Do you want to know GOD? Yes, you do. In this life, people say that there is more than one way to know GOD, because they have not been deeply rooted in the truth. If you were to ask GOD to give you an understanding, and you have faith that He will give you understanding, do you think that a loving GOD will let you down after seeking Him and wanting to know Him?

No, He will not because this is what He wants, and that's His love. He wants every man in heaven, but there are people who choose not to listen, so they are destroyed by their rejection of Him. First off, there must be a self-will in you, yourself. How can we be rewarded in heaven, as the Bible says, if we don't play a part in our choices of life? You play a part in our choices of life. You play a part in putting your roots deep in the Lord. The Lord gives us the strength, but we play the part of putting our faith in the Lord, and because of that choice, His spirit strengthens our spirit. "My son, don't forget my teachings. Remember what I tell you. What I teach will give you a good, long life and all will go well for you" (Proverbs 3:1–8).

His words give us long life. This next verse is the key to long life "Don't ever let love and loyalty leave you" (verse 3). That means we should always prove our love for the Lord through obedience, and we should always remain loyal to GOD and committed to what He says. To prove your love for GOD, you need to love people, and even your enemies—you must treat them fair. Write these things on your heart, and GOD will be pleased of you and so will most believers. You should never depend on your own knowledge. It is what He says about this situation. In every step you take you should have GOD on your agenda, and this brings deep roots. You should ask yourself, would GOD be pleased with this? The spirit will help you go the right way. This does not mean that you won't make mistakes; you will make mistakes, but in those mistakes, don't give up, continue to trust the Lord and He will help you.

Seeking after Him brings medicine to your body. If you have a sickness, begin to put your roots deep in Him and watch that sickness fade away. Love the Lord. Look for Him.

One thing that we make a mistake at is our longing for GOD to move. "Blessed are they which do hunger and thirst after righteousness: for they shall be filled" (Matthew 5:6). This tells me that if I thirst and hunger after Him, He will show up. Through the spirit of GOD, He will give you a hunger and then fill it. Put those things aside that waste your time and give GOD time in prayer.

GOD wants to prove Himself. Just think about if you were on a treasure hunt and you were being led by a treasure map, and every time you follow the map to a point, you find what you are looking for as the map directs you. Would that build you up to continue in your pursuit? Yes, it will, and that's the way GOD leads you.

Our Father will give you a rhema word and send your weariness another way. All this comes from trusting in GOD. This is what the Lord says, "Bad things will happen to those who put their trust in people. Bad things will happen to those who put their trust in human strength. There are laws of man and there are laws of GOD. We only follow man when we know that they are following GOD" (Jeremiah 17:5–7).

The Bible states that every man shall give account of himself to GOD (Romans 14:12); this means that on the day of judgment, it will be only you and GOD, and everyone else will be in line awaiting their turn to be judged. When we listen to Him, this carries His power, His anointing, His protection; and this puts our roots deep because we learn that He is truly dependable. "They will know that the Lord will do what He says" (verse 7). Now that's powerful!

STAYING CONNECTED

The second you disconnect from GOD, you start to wither. Do an experiment. Go outside and break a small limb from a tree and watch what happens to the leaves on that limb. They will start to wither. The same will happen to us if we stop reading our Bibles and seeking after wisdom. We are the branches and the Lord is the vine, so we have to stay connected to Him. When you feel like not reading, let your self-will kick in and take your hand and reach around to the back of your collar and pull up and say, "Let's go! You are going to read this Bible, even if you don't want to [lol]."

Put GOD first. When people begin to see your progress, it will change some of them to study, and this is the work that He has for each of us. It's no longer just the priests that are at work for GOD, it's also those sitting right in the pews with the same spirit as the preacher and that same power. GOD's spirit is being poured out upon all flesh, and this spirit helps mold you into Jesus.

How can a man, nailed to a cross, in all that pain, look at the people that did this and say, "Father, forgive them"? Under the influence of the spirit of GOD. Once they see Jesus in you, they will see a whole new perception of love and can't help but to glorify the GOD of heaven just because of you.

SET APART TO MAINTAIN DEPTH

Do you want to know the real definition to the word *stupid*? To follow people and their ways to hell *just to be* liked. What if GOD was to tell you to obey only what He says, how quick do you think you would make your first mistake? Now you see why Jesus is needed as your righteousness while you correct your ways. The biggest mistake we make in this life is to work to be accepted by man.

We should never work to be accepted by man, but we should work to be obedient to GOD. Disobedience brings rejection, rejection that has you sometimes feeling alone and out of touch with the real world, and that is just where GOD wants His people to be, not conformed to this world because it adds no value to heaven's calling. Heaven's calling is a place where GOD's presence abides. His presence is His spirit, and in His spirit is where His authority is. "If we walk in the light, as He is in the light" (1 John 1:7). The Easy Read Version says this: "We should live in the light where GOD is."

When I first became a Christian, I never realized that I was going to learn about how much the church has to learn. We still have a long way to go in the reality of being Christ-like. I've seen spiritual leaders seek to use their powers to kill and think that it is justified by GOD.

When we get into that sway to please man, we have to maintain our membership by showing love to who they want you to love and showing hate to who they want you to hate, and the minute you don't show approval to what they want, you are disqualified and become a spectacle, which means that you are now a traitor.

Now they are watching your every move to see if you are working against them. Can you see now, how GOD knows what they will do? He uses that and you to show them how it is supposed to be done. He uses their own hearts and ways to guide them to watch you. "For the wisdom of this world is foolishness with GOD. For it is written: He taketh the wise in their own craftiness" (1 Corinthians 3:19).

Again, the Lord knows the thoughts of the wise, and they are vain or worth nothing. We see how when we set ourselves apart and do what GOD says, we truly become wise. The spirit of GOD and His nutrition takes your root deep to where you now stand as GOD Himself, not that you are GOD, but your actions carry GOD's authority and power—a power that cannot be denied by no man.

Your actions are GOD's actions, therefore GOD Himself is moving through you just like He moved through Jesus. The reason GOD was so pleased with Him was because He said Himself that He did only what He saw His Father do. If He is our example, then we seek to do only what we see GOD do.

Know GOD and move. *Sanctified* means to be set apart for GOD's use. We should all put ourselves in a position where GOD can use us. You can be used by Satan, or you can choose to be used by GOD. Jesus said that He came to destroy the works of the Devil. All the things Satan loves to do (steal, kill, destroy), Satan could not use Him, not one time.

Do you run with people in this life using these methods to get through life? Then you are being used by Satan. Do you really think that some other person or persons are in your way that you have to exercise what Satan does in order for you to prosper? Are you kidding me? I speak from a spiritual point of view, knowing that GOD Himself can bring you to where you need to be as long as you are set apart for GOD. Trust me when I say that GOD knows how to make things work on His behalf.

He knows how to make it work and move people on your behalf. Where we fall off is where we don't trust GOD in all things, and if we don't trust Him in whatever it is, it is not entitled to His power. That's where we start to worry, by not being in subjection to GOD in whatever it is. If your roots are deep in GOD, you are not easily moved or plucked up because a persuasion is a wind of doctrine that comes your way that is not of GOD, but from an evil force that tries to move what you know about the Father. That is why when we read the Scripture, you should allow the word of GOD to sink in by meditation of truth. This is what brings your roots deep, by being deep in truth even when you don't fully get why He wants you to do something that you don't understand.

This is where our trust in GOD is rooted, because we see Him move, and the only thing we did was had faith in GOD that He will do what He says.

There was a man whom the Bible calls our Father of Faith. In other words, GOD used him as the founder of our beliefs in spiritual promises. He and his wife were old in age and both knew in reality that they were too old to have a child. But GOD spoke and told them that they would have a child. Watch how he and his wife put their roots deep. They fully rejected what they knew about themselves and their wombs and just believed what GOD said, giving glory to Him as a finished promise.

This is where GOD Himself entered her womb, as He did the Mother of Jesus, and brought forth a son. But the spirit that I get is that it was Abraham himself that was fully trusting GOD. "He staggered not at the *promise of GOD* through unbelief; but was strong in faith, giving glory to GOD [deep roots]; and being *fully persuaded* [deep roots] that what he [GOD] had promised, he [GOD] was able to perform" (Romans 4:20-21).

That tells us that no matter what the circumstance is, we should meditate continually on what the Father says, and this is what brings us into full persuasion that the Father will move. Now that's power, by just trusting GOD and depositing and cultivating what He says in your heart.

Even though we receive the word of GOD, that root is the Holy Spirit Himself and how you in yourself, cultivate His truth in you. "They on the rock are they, which, when they hear, receive the word with joy; and these have no root, which for a while believe, and in time of temptation fall away" (Luke 8:13).

Men fall away from GOD for only two reasons. For not having the Holy Spirit that is given by accepting Christ Jesus, or they purposely don't put their roots deep into what GOD the Father says. Spend time in GOD's word, study Jesus Himself, and trust me, you won't be moved.

GOD'S FORGIVENESS

Whatever mentality you have for others when they sin is the same you will have for yourself. If you continue to hold grudges against people because they sin, the second you do something wrong, you will continue to be condemned and will hold a grudge against yourself because that's the way you deal with sin. Never let the Devil keep you focused on him. That is why some don't feel saved or don't feel forgiven of past sins because they hold other people at bay. That is the reason some people lose their life prematurely because you let doctrines of devils hinder the work of the spirit in your life where he can't keep you because of the way you handle others.

Forgive, and you shall be forgiven. Do not condemn others, and you shall not be condemned. You must be at the point to where the spirit of GOD can flow and cleanse you of sin first, then sickness and evil. Forgiveness is a must when it comes to being healed. All of GOD's children must maintain a heart of forgiveness.

Even in pain, we must learn how to forgive. Most people don't want to even think about forgiving a person, or persons, when the pain is fresh. But that is where you can experience the most power of GOD, because it is He who helps you to do right. Like Jesus on the cross, inside tremendous pain is when He forgave, so if He was our example, then we are able to forgive.

Let me fill you in on something, when you refuse to forgive what you are doing, you are telling GOD that He can't use you at that moment. The most powerful person on earth is the one who allows GOD to do what He wants through them. The deepest forgiver is the one who is identified with Christ. Revelation start to flow at deep forgiveness, and you start to understand Jesus Himself; you start to understand the Father. That is how you become to know Him by putting yourself in His shoes, and the Holy Spirit begins to teach you things many people don't know, just because you chose to exceed in your forgiveness of others. The deeper you forgive in GOD's glory, the deeper your communion with GOD.

It is your choice to seek to please the Father. GOD was able to work through Jesus 100 percent, that is why He had so much power; when He spoke, things moved. All you have to say is "Not my will, but your will GOD." In other words, you will be saying to GOD, "Not what I want to do by holding a grudge, but what you want me to do and the Holy Spirit will strengthen your spirit to carry out this process." GOD is love. "Love seeketh not her own" (1 Corinthians 13:5). When you love your enemy, you don't seek your own will; you seek GOD's own: "thinketh no evil" (verse 5).

Your efforts toward that person should show that there is no grudge, even though you still remember what they did. You may even feel in your flesh that that person thinks you are a weak person or a person that they can mishandle when they get ready, but later in this chapter, I'm going to show you that that's when the judgment of GOD is nearer—when you seek to forgive, because you have denied yourself and GOD Himself is present. Your enemy is no longer doing you wrong; now it is GOD they are doing wrong. Your flesh will not receive this, but your spirit will, and you will get to the point where people can't easily make you angry. The Bible states that a person who gets angry easily is a fool. This is a process that GOD is working in you so you must learn how to take up this cross every day, as GOD gives you strength. Remain close to GOD and learn how to submit to GOD, then your spirit man becomes the front runner in your life and the one that is doing the works of GOD.

Vengeance belongs to GOD, and your angels are always at the face of GOD, ready to protect you (Matthew 18:10). Whatever type of action you dish out to others is what you bring on yourself. If you are a person of forgiveness, then when you do something wrong, GOD forgives you. If you are a person of vengeance, then when you miss the mark, you are vindicated.

All of us fall at times, but you are becoming a new person. "Put on the new man, which is renewed in the knowledge after the image of Him that created him" (Colossians 3:10). Your new man is trained after what we know about Jesus Christ Himself, how He functioned with others and how He loved.

We know that He forgave everyone that did Him wrong— everyone. "Put on therefore, as the elect of GOD, holy and beloved, bowels of mercies, kindness, humbleness of mind, meekness, long suffering. Forbearing one another, and forgiving one another, if any man has a quarrel against any: [watch this] even as Christ forgave you, so also do ye" (verse 12–13).

When you function this way, those whose eyes are open can see Jesus Himself through you, and this forces men and women to look up and glorify GOD by your good works. We don't want to make GOD look like a destructive GOD; we want to make Him look like who He is.

Some people have people saying things about the Father because of the way they claim to be a child of GOD, but at the same time, they're acting like a child of the devil. What would Jesus look like standing, preaching, and slandering other preachers? His duty was not to harm men and women, but to bring them out of sin, and the person who delivers pain and words of abuse is the one that is really ignored. (Forgiveness.)

Who wants to be in subjection to the one that delivers pain? But we all want to get away from an oppressive person. We are delivered from oppression and captivity in Christ Jesus.

SEATED

When a person is forgiven of a sin through the death of Christ Jesus who sits at the right hand of GOD, then that person who has been forgiven is also seated at GOD's right hand as if he has done no wrong in GOD's eyes. We, as men and women of GOD, have received everything GOD has for us, but the problem is our belief. We don't truly believe, and that's why we don't receive instantly.

Our minds should always go to the fact that Jesus is forever interceding for us. In other words, whatever we ask for, Jesus, in His holy innocence, speaks to the Father on our behalf. If we are at GOD's right hand, then what person can stand against us as believers. That person who truly believes that Jesus has cleansed them of all sins, then that person has Jesus's death, burial, and resurrection on His behalf and is truly set free.

With that being said, listen to what the scriptures says about receiving from GOD. "He [GOD] that spared not his own Son, but delivered him up for us all, how shall He not *with* Him also freely give us all things" (Romans 8:32). Our problem is, we are in tune to how man operates a function to forgiveness. "Freely" means that we don't have to do anything but believe. Being prone to human beliefs, we think we have to do something to get it. There's just one thing we have to do, and that is to go and get or act out what GOD has given.

If you have committed sin last week and you have asked GOD to forgive you, the Bible states that GOD throws that sin into a sea of forgetfulness

(Jeremiah 31). If GOD has forgotten it, then there is nothing in His sight that holds us back from it. Who can accuse you of sin, if GOD has forgiven it? Of course, you know that there will be some that still remember what you did, and these are the ones that give us trouble in feeling forgiven of that sin.

Let me ask you this one thing, whose side is GOD on at this point? Yours! If GOD has forgotten your sin, then the person who is still accusing you of sin is in danger of GOD, because he doesn't remember. That's why the Bible goes on to say this: "Who shall lay anything to the charge of GOD's elect? It is GOD who justifieth" (Romans 8:33).

Now let me read that from Romans 8:33–34 (ERV): "Who can accuse the people GOD has chosen? No one! Who can say that GOD's people are guilty?" No one! GOD allows people against us to exercise our beliefs in Christ. Because you know that when they come against us, then we have to wrestle against their principality and power with a deliberate act to keep ourselves in the truth, therefore choosing Christ. Their principalities and powers are directly against the truth of grace and the realities of the resurrected Christ. We are fighting against their way of thinking.

CLEANSED

We as forgiven saints, must set ourselves in this life in a way to maintain and generate the fact that we are forgiven and clean from all unrighteousness. If you say that you are forgiven, then you must continue at GOD boldly to His throne believing for those things Jesus died for. Your faith in GOD and you continuously pleading for justice proves that you believe. Listen to what Jesus says about a person who never lets go of what he/she believes. He gives an illustration of a worldly leader first, then He goes on to say that GOD will even more when we continue as a person who takes time every day to pray to GOD.

The very fact that you have been cleansed means that there are no sins pending—not one. If there are no sins pending, there should be nothing in between you and GOD to receive from GOD. Of course, you know that even when you are clean in GOD's eyes, some people still won't see eye to eye with GOD. In their eyes, they still have that sin fresh in their mind. Through your continuous standing before the throne of GOD for justice, He sometimes allows judgment to those whose actions art still according to past sins. If you stand by and never pray or start praying then stop, then something you will go without, as if you are still guilty of that sin.

Yes, it goes just like that. If you sit back and never produce a prayer life, then through this worlds' system, you will be held accountable against past sins because of your unbelief that GOD will give you justice. You can't weary GOD by your continuous prayers to Him like the lady in this chapter. You will actually please GOD because He longs to be trusted.

In Luke 18:1–8, the Bible states that this judge didn't fear GOD. That tells me that his decision was not according to GOD, but because this lady that stayed on His mind, He gave her justice. We know that GOD Himself goes beyond anything man does so listen to what it says in verse 7–8, "Shall not GOD avenge [give justice] His own elect, which cry day and night unto Him, though He bear long with them? I will tell you that He will avenge them speedily [quickly]."

This judge was unjust, the Bible states. In order for a judge to be just, every decision that he makes has to be according to the Cross for which there is total forgiveness. That makes it nearly impossible for them to be just because they operate and decide according to evidence.

But GOD operates according to His son and those who are in His son. Those who are in His son are totally forgiven, are clean. Glory to GOD. This cleanliness is a deliberate act that you as a child of GOD have to clothe yourself within. Then it's a mind frame that Christ gives of Himself. Totally legal through submission and subjection to Christ. "Put on therefore as the elect of GOD" (Colossians 3:12). Put on? Put on? Put on what? Put on Christ! Listen to what it identifies who Christ is, so go ahead right now and frame your mind to what you are about to hear "Put on therefore, as the elect of GOD, *holy* and *beloved, bowels of mercies, kindness, humbleness of mind, meekness, longsuffering*" (verse 12).

This is who you are. This is what you do. This proves that you are cleansed from that old ugly person you used to be. In order to maintain cleanliness, you must practice these on all men because this is how Christ is toward you. You must continue to allow Him to show Himself to others through you, through subjecting the Holy Spirit to the brethren. "For bearing one another, and forgiving one another, if any man have a quarrel against any" (verse 13).

Listen to this last part that commands us to let Christ reign through us. "Even as Christ forgave you, so also do ye." When you do this, brother, you allow the Holy Spirit to constantly cleanse you, because if there is a flow of spirit, just as water, dirt, or filth, can never build. But when you stop allowing the spirit to flow out from you, filth builds and stagnation builds, and our old man begins to take control again. That old man that is entitled to judgments. Maintain your forgiveness and maintain your cleanliness, and the GOD of heaven will be pleased with you.

WITCHCRAFT AND ITS ROLE IN BELIEVERS

First of all, let's define the word *witchcraft*. In past times, we have had many ways of how we determine what witchcraft is. The first thing we think of is coming from a childhood story. We think about a witch flying through the air on a broom, trying to scare you. The definition of witchcraft is "(1) The use of sorcery or magic; (2) Intercourse with the devil or with familiar spirits; (3) An irresistible influence or fascination."

In the Webster's Dictionary, it suggests some ways that there is an evil influence involved. That is on target.

So let's go to the Bible and bring it in to focus. "Rebellion is as the sin of witchcraft and stubbornness is as iniquity and idolatry" (1 Samuel 15:23). Let's look at each part of the scriptures. First, the words *rebellion* and *witchcraft* are alike. There is a reason the Bible puts the word *rebellion* first. We all know that word means opposition to one in authority or dominance. If we oppose someone in authority, that's rebellion and witchcraft. It becomes witchcraft because ones opposition sends a message to control that person in authority and the situation.

Most of the time, we need to be careful about how we view one who rebels. Because that person may rebel against unlawful control, and that, my friend, is not witchcraft. Jesus was rebellious against the religious leaders of His time. This is why they crucified Him, because He would not operate the ways they demanded.

Only when those who you oppose are right and not against the spirit of GOD. Now let's see when a person is in witchcraft and rebel against GOD. "Love your enemies, bless them that curse you, do good to them that hate you and pray for them which despitefully use you and persecute you" (Matthew 5:44).

Now you have gotten the true word of GOD, and if you are not doing good to your enemy, then you are in rebellion of witchcraft. You want to control your own situation, but Jesus Himself wants to control the situation. That's witchcraft against the Son of GOD. Jesus is commanding you to love, and if you love, then you partake of GOD and His spirit. But rebellion is always another spirit that is of the human nature. Humanity says that if you hit me, I will hit you. If you say something about me, I will get you later and get the hell out of my face.

Every obedience to GOD is allowing Him to handle the problem. When we disobey, we are telling the Father, "I got it, I know better than you. My way will work, but yours won't. Can you see how Satan has taken over?" Don't run with witches, run with GOD. There are a lot of controlling people who are churchgoers and even in this world. But no one has the right to oppress and control people. We have righteous laws to handle the ones that go off track. But as far as witchcraft is concerned, we should allow people to express their own calling that only they know what they desire for GOD. If a person wants to sing, don't try to force him/her to become a pastor. If he wants to play ball, don't try to force him to be a doctor, because Satan, in all his rebellion against GOD, wants to keep us from the place GOD has called us to, even though GOD is with us in everything we do by faith. We won't have full power and potential until we get to that place GOD called us to.

Growing up as a young boy, I always loved music. There is something about music that energizes me. As a young boy, I bought a system to play music, a disc jockey. We had a secular group called Sypho. When we played, we became popular in our city during the times of disco, and skating was very popular at that time. We had sold out skating where the fire marshal had to lock the doors to keep more from entering for fear that too many people would not be able to exit in time if there was danger. After many years studying music and how people respond to music and its lyrics, I learned a lot. After hearing my mother for years talk about Jesus, I gave up my DJ gigs and sold all my equipment to one in the group who continued to play. My mind was that my love for music will not be denied. So I started to listen to gospel music, and when I did, I discovered that gospel music had a big impact on my culture.

Here's the deal about just the instruments of music. When an instrument is played, no matter how you play it or what beat you make, it can only be expressed against GOD until the lyrics come in. If you glorify GOD, then whatever beat you have doesn't matter because it's Him that's on your mind. Just as in preaching, some lyrics carry a big impact of anointing and some don't, depending on one speaking; and every culture and ethnicity have their own style of music. To win people in that culture to Christ in secular music, I learned that the lyrics drove the young people into what was being said, but now we have music with the same type of culture, but with lyrics that glorifies the GOD of heaven.

So now I have a new system where I play, and GOD is able to reach some of the same people, but with the gospel just as bold as I was in secular music. Now I am even bolder by the spirit of GOD playing music. But just like Christ, some people will oppose you. The people in my city saw me play secular music, but now play gospel. These are some who are now into witchcraft against my music. You have to know that when we first started this chapter, I gave you a definition of *witchcraft*. It talks about sorcery and familiar spirits. Familiar spirits are what was against Christ when He went back to His hometown. You see, they are familiar with you because they know you, and instead of them releasing the Holy Spirit, they release familiar spirits at you and at the people.

The Bible states that Jesus could not function properly in His own town. These spirits work against you and what you do. This is how Satan uses his people against GOD's people, even some Christians, which is not supposed to be. From what I get from how Jesus treated His followers and disciples was with respect. Through witchcraft, there can be much damage done as far as trusting each other. We should respect each other's calling.

The religious leaders of the time of Jesus Christ judged Him wrong, and they were certainly opposing Him at His calling. I saw many people bring GOD's judgment upon themselves through the ignorance of witchcraft, thinking that the heart of their judgment was right. "The wise heart will receive Commandments: but a prating fool shall fall" (Proverbs 10:8). Even though we run into evil men, GOD is still the vindicator. When you are in your calling, there is a force field of protection, and the forcefield is the Holy Spirit. Through witchcraft, many people have fallen away from what they were really called to do when the GOD of heaven longs for them to move. Now when they allow these spirits to operate in a community, they can become widespread and have them working through a human agenda, therefore spreading through many people in one city. That's why Jesus commanded His disciples that "when they persecute you in one city, flee ye to another" (Matthew 10:23), because witchcraft starts to take over and your influences weakened. That is if you are truly ministering the force of the gospel of grace, which is what Satan doesn't want, because he can't work from grace. He can only work through oppression, which is what witchcraft is. A force to make you submit to it through an unconscious or self-willed decision, through ignorance.

When the Holy Spirit is released from a prophet of GOD, there is no force against GOD's will, only comfort to allow a person to make a willful decision to obey GOD. That's the only way it becomes legal for righteousness. By self-will, GOD hates these spirits operating in this world, especially among His people. He calls these spirits an abomination. "When thou art come unto the land which the Lord thy GOD giveth thee, thou shalt not learn to do after the abominations of those nations. There shall not be found among you anyone that maketh his son or his daughter to pass through the fire, or that uses divination or an enchanter or a witch" (Deuteronomy 18:9–12). What GOD was saying here is that these other nations worship other gods and are pagan nations. Even in the Old Testament, the Holy Spirit was at work because GOD does not work outside of His spirit. The Holy Spirit is gentle and influences you to obey GOD, but these other spirits bring turmoil into your life in order to control your surroundings to force you into obedience to its agenda.

GOD told them not to learn from these other nations that cause their sons and daughters turmoil in order to bring subjection. This only gives them an impression of evil and gives them an evil conscience. I've learned that a person who abuses their children usually come from an abusive background. They learned from someone they were taught by. Because abuse or oppression opens a person's heart and life for these spirits to work.

Just think for one minute if you encounter two people, one blesses you and tells you jokes and makes you laugh. The second you meet that person again, you feel his spirit and want to joke and laugh. But the other person, every time you meet him, he takes a switch and raps you on the back. Would that person bring you a smile every time you encounter him? No, he will bring you to anger. Just think about a child or even adults when they receive abu-sive forces for a long period of time, they become familiar to those type of surroundings, and when they deliver discipline, they intend to think that that's how to deliver it. But with GOD, it's different. And what GOD was trying to do among the Israelites was to express Himself and His goodness, but throughout the Old Testament, GOD couldn't find one man to express Himself fully, even though He gave us many great prophets then. The Bible states that He came with grace and truth. He expressed the Father to full extent. There is a difference with this world's leadership than the leadership of Christ Jesus. Jesus commanded us not to use force like this world's system, but to be gentle and serve. Because grace opens the heart to receive the one distributing the grace.

There was a black lady that came to Jesus with her two sons, who desired to sit on Jesus's right hand of power when He sat in heaven. The heart of those two sons were to dominate people, but Jesus put them in the right perspective about heaven and the understanding of the love of GOD when people find out that all you want to do is dominate, they get angry.

The other disciples did just that, but Jesus called them all together and gave them an illustration of heaven's leadership. "But Jesus called them unto him and said, 'Ye know that the princes of the gentiles' exercise domination over them, and they are great exercise authority upon them, but it shall not be so among you: but whosoever will be great among you, let him be your minister'" (Matthew 20:25–28). The princes of the gentiles are the authorities of this world. Even though the Bible states that we are in this world, we are not of this world; we have a kingdom of operation. We operate like we are in heaven, or supposed to. Even though these men are in place for GOD's earthly government, they can also go beyond authority and entertain evil spirits and witchcraft. A person is deceived when he thinks that everything government officials do pleases GOD. They are also punished when they go beyond and entertain evil.

SIN IN THESE LAST DAYS

I understand that this is a chapter that we all are familiar with and do not want to talk about when it comes to sins of our own, because after all, who wants to see sin in themselves? Well, you are going to be surprised at this chapter because it only speaks about the human race, but everyone else is okay.

Let's go to where GOD gives us an understanding of sin, and humanity understands that the only reason GOD chose Noah and his family was because they were sinners just like everyone else, but the difference was that they chose not to practice sin. Even though we are all sinners, the only ones that can remain clean are the ones that chose not to practice sin. In Christ Jesus, it's not only claiming Him, but we also have to practice what He says. Of course, we all miss the mark at times, but when you notice yourself in the wrong, you have an obligation to Him to show that you appreciate the fact that He gave His life to take away that sin, and by turning away, you show proof of that. By submitting to Him, you give sin less power and authority in your life. Listen to what happened and how GOD saw sin in the human race. "Then the Lord saw the wickedness of man was great in the earth and that every intent of the thoughts of men's Hearts was only evil continually. The Lord was sorry that he had made man on Earth and He was grieved in His heart" (Genesis 6:5–6). GOD saw wickedness over the whole world, and people just didn't want to do right because my Bible tells me that Noah preached for 120 years. Just like some people do today, they ignore the fact that there will come a day when what is being preached will have to be heeded in order to be saved. At that time on earth, man really wasn't aware of how they were sinning until Moses, but GOD knew, and I truly believe that in these last days, it will be the same way. In these last days, there are things that people do that is wrong, and I'm not only talking about the world. I'm referring to some Bible-toters too. Willful sin is going to be ramped in broad daylight. Some believers will know for a fact, that person will be judged. "Remember that some people lead sinful lives and everyone knows that they will be judged. But there are others whose sin will not be revealed until later" (1 Timothy 5:24).

When I read this verse, I asked GOD, "Why will some people's will be revealed later?" And this is what he revealed to me, "You see, when we deal with people every day, there must be true love flowing from our hearts, and the second we do not allow GOD's love to flow through us to that other person, you are in sin, and for the very fact, you have cut GOD off and are now functioning from your own human self or some evil spirit. GOD is GOD, and He is not like us because everything GOD does is perfect and just. That means, in order for us to be perfect, we have to tap into Him and His way. The Bible states that GOD is love; that means everything He does is to express His love for us. We look at it different when we run into difficulties concerning someone else. We don't want to stand and continue to love and become perfect like GOD.

GOD is love; listen to what the Bible says about love. When we read about love, I want you to put GOD in the place of the word *love*, and that will give you a view of the cross of Jesus Christ. "Love [GOD] worketh no ill to his neighbor" (Romans 13:10). That's saying that GOD does no wrong to anyone New Living Translation. So, in essence, that's what we must do. Remember, it says "no ill."

Not one thing should we do wrong to one person, and if we do, we are in sin. Can you see why the righteousness of Christ is needed? Because if you didn't have His righteousness, just one sin sends you to the slammer. The remaining of that verse says that "love is fulfilling of the law," meaning perfect. In other words, love satisfies all of GOD's requirements. And if you look around like I do, starting with myself, just about everyone was doing wrong.

Some people were accusing me of things that I wasn't doing. Some people, actually at that time, were calling me gay because their point was that a person who goes around not having sex must be gay.

How absurd is that, them knowing that I was a Christian? They act like GOD can't keep you and control your desires. At times, I felt like running to the first girl that was sweet on me and throw her down on the bed, just to prove myself. Then I thought, wait a minute, I know I'm not gay, so what do I have to prove to them? Then the Holy Spirit spoke. "This is just temptation to push you into sin." I just brushed if off and was led to the scriptures, where it says, "All who live Godly shall suffer persecution" (2 timothy 3:12).

To talk about sin, when that kind of pressure hit, GOD starts to reveal things to you about Christ and retaliation because if I would have fought back, even that would put me into sin. And I understood that this is how He felt when pressure was put on Him, but He wasn't moved by the pressure. For some reason, we become like the Bible states, a city on a hill or a spectacle. Through no retaliation, many in the church can see that they have been sinning against GOD.

Because it is getting closer to time, I believe that the Father is separating the sheep from the goats through pressure of taking up our crosses. You know that the spirit of the cross or the spirit of Jesus, let GOD express His love to all men through no retaliation. The pressure is on, and the fire burns up everything that is not like the cross. This is where the fake people will remain in church but continue to sin and hate because they can clearly see that it takes commitment to endure. "Sin will be rampant everywhere, and the love of many will grow cold" (Matthew 24:9–13). Talking about some people in church, when we teach Christ, many will deny Him by not loving that other person. Now, don't get me wrong, I'm not here to point out anyone's sin, but I'm only here to prove all our needs to submit to Jesus and not to man, because in submission to man over GOD, it carries zero power to overcome sin. We have to acknowledge Him in this world, and when we see where we can express His love, then we must move on that very fact.

Let me tell you a story Christ told to explain how we should function. This is what I want you to grab ahold of—these men we claim to be Godly, but expressed negligence where love was badly needed. "A Jewish man was traveling on a trip from Jerusalem to Jericho, and he was attacked by bandits. They stripped him of his clothes and money and beat him and left him half dead beside the road. By chance, a Jewish priest came along, but when he saw the man lying there, he crossed to the other side of the road and passed by him" (Luke 10:30–37).

Now let's look at this, a priest is one who carries GOD with him, and he saw a helpless man and saw clearly that the man needed help, but he kept going. If you look at what really happened, you will see that GOD left that man to die on the side of the road, not because he wanted to, but because that priest would not let GOD help through His authority. This man rejected love. To tell the truth, this man rejected GOD dwelling in him. Because I found out that when we clearly see a need and don't move, we reject GOD, point blank! "If any of you have enough money to live well, and see a brother or sister in need and refuses to help—how can GOD's love dwell in that person?" (1 John 3:17).

You see where sin is. It is not allowing GOD to help love through your expression. Yet there was a good Samaritan that came along and supplied everything the man needed. Then Jesus pointed out the good Samaritan and commanded His disciples to do the same. He may not have known that passing by the hurt man, but one thing I found out is that unknown sin is not that damaging until we find out that it is sin by the law. That sin gets its strength by you knowing that it is wrong.

Now the Holy Spirit is asking us to do what is right by all men. But even if you do, Jesus becomes our, what the Bible calls, propitiation. The word *propitiate* and *propitiation* are not commonly used in the English language. We must look to an age long gone in order to discern their meaning. In ancient times, many Polytheists thought of their gods as unpredictable beings, liable to become angry with their worshipers for any trifle or wasting. When any misfortune occurred, it was believed that a god was angry and was therefore punishing his worshipers. The remedy was to offer the god a sacrifice to appease his anger. The process was called propitiation. Well, we have a propitiation for our sins. One who appeases the true god's anger. His name is Jesus. Whenever GOD's children sin, they provoke His anger, but of course, GOD's anger is not an irrational lack of self-control, as it so often is with humans. His anger is the settled opposition of His holy nature to all evil, and when He gets angry, we cannot stop judgments with just a "hello" and "you have pretty eyes."

The Bible tells us that only through the cross of Christ can GOD's anger be appeased. Because he was a man that pleased GOD perfectly, and get this, if you are identified with Him, then you please GOD perfectly. Now His death on the cross was for every man in this entire world that ever lived (1 John 2:2). Now this is not the only way we see Jesus on the cross. But the cross is what the Bible states: GOD demonstrated His love to us by sending His Son to become the propitiation for our sins. Christ's death brings us back into fellowship with GOD for all who accept Him. Simplicity of the gospel of Christ is the fact that sin separates us from GOD, and Jesus brings us back to Him because of His non-sinful body.

To give you an understanding of what you do is that you attach your soul to His body, rejecting to practice sin, and GOD qualifies you as sinless. In other words, you are now part of Jesus, but sins that you do willfully cannot be covered because of your agreement to do them. GOD wants you to keep your faith cultivated and apply pressure against sin. By doing so, you give GOD permission to remove sin from your body and soul. Because you give the Holy Spirit permission to do His work in you. This is what the Bible calls holiness. By you giving GOD full access or control of your entire being, this pleases Him.

GOD IS YOUR FATHER

GOD will not do anything in you without your permission. It is the same with evil desires. You can give your desires permission to work, and they become strong or you cannot give them permission to work, even though you may be applying them at a certain level, but by your choice to not do them, they become weaker. That is how the desire to sin is destroyed. If you keep that one fact that there has to be a willful consciousness to reject sin, you are on your way to become what the Bible calls holy.

HOLINESS

First off, let me explain holiness and righteousness because there is a difference. Righteousness is what Christ purchased for us, bringing us back to GOD, and it is an area where no man could have done because there could not be present, not one sin, even from birth; therefore His righteous body is able to be with GOD and commune with GOD because of His Holiness. But holiness for you is a choice and, on your part, to maintain in the sight of GOD.

Just because you have received Jesus Christ as Lord, you are righteous, and that's done and settled. Now by your choice, you have to maintain Him (holiness), and it expels the consciousness of sin. By you knowing that you are right with GOD through Him, this gives you power to do right. Believe it or not, your holiness has nothing to do with present sins in you but has everything to do with a forward movement to please GOD, because of His goodness that saved you from your sins. "But as He which hath called you is holy, so be ye holy in all manner of conversation" (1 Peter 1:15).

The word *conversation* is universal. It means "conduct or behavior," and your conduct and behavior are in your doings—it is in your speeches, it is in how you handle money, how you treat your wife/ husband. Your holiness is how you conduct yourself before GOD first. You see, that's a big mistake we all make in life—trying to please man first—and by you trying to please man first, you have no power from GOD because of wrong subjection. You are more conscious of man than you are GOD, therefore your faith to be holy is not in GOD or is secondary, so GOD has no right to energize you full to become holy even though the Holy Spirit is right there in you. Because we must subject ourselves to the Father just as He says and the way He says. This is not legalism nor does it have anything to do with being legalized.

You see, GOD is Himself. He never changes, and He is the only true GOD. Therefore, if you are going to receive from your Father, you must commune with Him. Remember at the start of this chapter, I said that you become part of Christ's Holy Body. When I say *body*, I don't mean His people; I mean Him, His physical body. If any limb of your body becomes detached, how can that limb receive your blood flow? How can your brain tell it to move? It can't, and it dies not being attached.

With the Father, it's the same. There are ways and actions of heaven, and there are ways and actions of man. When you subject yourself to the ways and actions of GOD by faith in GOD, you become GOD Himself, through oneness, and your Father GOD will have it no other way than oneness. Then true holiness is a purehearted subjection to the Father through Christ Jesus. "For with GOD nothing shall be impossible" (Luke 1:37).

This is not talking about just your accepting of GOD; this is talking about your subjecting to the ways of His spirit and what GOD says and does, so because your heart is pure when you speak, GOD has spoken; and when GOD speaks, things move, things are created, even demons move when GOD/you speak.

Now you see why holiness is important in your life. It is for your actions and ways to not be denied in His pure *unadulterated* power of the Holy Spirit. Now obey your Father. "Because it is written, be ye holy; for I am holy" (1 Peter 1:16).

Now this book's definition of holiness: Actions and ways not being mixed with nothing but the Father God.

HEAVEN'S AUTHORITY

Before we get into this chapter, let's define the word *authority* and keep it fresh in our minds throughout this chapter. In Webster's Dictionary, it says, "Power to influence or command; person in command; a convincing force." This means that a person in authority has power to do what he/she has power to do. In this kind of authority, human authority, a mother or father has power over their children, a teacher has power over her class, or a police officer has power to stop a car when the law is broken.

Now I know that some may see these as supreme authorities. Every one of these should be in subjection to supreme authority. In the presence of GOD's authority, there is a presence that must be reverenced or GOD Himself will bring judgment to any person or group. When GOD is ignored and power is abused, GOD Himself snatches any other authority or power from the atmosphere through Righteous Judgement. The second judgment falls, attention is turned to heaven, and by the time you get to the end of this chapter, you will know about the Father and have a reverential fear of GOD that brings His presence to you for protection.

It's not when you fear GOD that brings judgment; it's when you don't fear GOD that you go through life as if He is not watching your every move, but when you fear Him, you are in vigilant choice of right and wrong. If the Father didn't let us know when we do wrong as a people, we would go about this life and never come to know Him and accept His offer to heaven.

In GOD's presence, the atmosphere changes and GOD takes control of all abilities. I often wondered why the Bible stated that one day, (every) knee shall bow and (every) tongue shall confess that Jesus is Lord. We know that there are all kinds of people from the beginning of time until now. Some of which have been ruled totally evil and even hate GOD, and if they could, they would have nothing to do with GOD. How do you get a person that is totally evil to bow down and confess? You get them to bow down and confess by supreme authority who controls the atmosphere and even the air we breathe. (GOD's authority that is of heaven rules even when executed by humans.) When Jesus walked this earth, heaven's authority walked this earth and also man's authority walked this earth at the same time. He executed heaven's full ability, and that's why He was so powerful. Through the first man, Adam, GOD gave him authority to rule this earth. (You know the story of Adam and Eve.)

But one day, human authority will expire, and all that will be left is heaven's authority. The Bible states that when Christ comes back, he will do away with all authority. That means that any earthly authority does not belong to or rules inside of GOD's kingdom. "Then cometh the end, when he shall have delivered up the Kingdom of GOD, even the Father; when he shall have put down all rule and all authority and power" (1 Corinthians 15:24).

You have to think about the fact that what will we need for police in heaven? There will be no evildoers. Why would we need a president? We have Christ Jesus on His throne and the Father. These authorities are only for earth and belongs to earth. But even at times they abuse power, GOD Himself has to step in for the love of humanity, even His people, especially His people.

There was a man that went about killing the people of GOD in the Old Testament. He hated GOD's people with a passion. His name was Saul.

I know for a fact that there was a cry coming from the people of GOD against this man's authority. But the problem was that he thought that by killing them, he was doing what pleases GOD. He was on the right track by wanting to please GOD, but using the wrong action and defeating the purpose. He encountered GOD Himself (Jesus).

If Jesus is seated at the right hand of GOD in power, then when He functioned, He functioned directly from the Father. When Saul met Jesus on the road to Damascus, some say that Jesus knocked him to the ground, but let me tell you the truth of the matter. The presence of the Father snatched His authority from him. He knew in that helpless state, lying on his back, that a source hit him, and he lost all his ability, even in his mind. When he fell to the ground, he automatically called Him Lord.

As you read, notice how when light appears darkness flees. "And Saul yet breathing out threatening and slaughter against the disciples of the Lord, went unto the Priest and desired of him, letters to Damascus to the Synagogues, that if he found any of this way, whether they were men or women, he might bring them bound unto Jerusalem. And as he journeyed, he came near Damascus; and suddenly there shined round about him, a light from Heaven. And he fell to the earth and heard a voice saying unto him, 'Saul, Saul, why persecute thou me?' He said, 'Who art though Lord?' And he said, 'I am Jesus whom thou persecute. It is hard for thee to kick against the pricks.' He trembled and was astonished and said, 'Lord, what will thou have me to do?' The Lord said, 'Arise and go unto the city and it shall be told thee what thou must do'" (Acts 9:1–6).

Now the rest of the story tells that Saul became a preacher from that very moment and had nothing else to do with darkness.

I tell you this as wisdom: Saul, even in his evil actions, acknowledged GOD, so when we acknowledge GOD in what we do by submission, the Father knows how to bring us to the right action. If Saul would have been a servant of men in his authority, he probably would have lost his life through wrong submission.

Because in all we do as members of this earth, it must be GOD over men, or you are in a dangerous position. Because of GOD's love for all humans, His authority is always in the light. If we walk in the light and have love for all humans, then you will have GOD's presence and His ability. In GOD's presence, devils know the presence of GOD because the light shines on evil and brings it out in the open to see. When a man like Jesus walks up, the first thing that devils feel is GOD, and in His presence, they can't move around like they can in darkness, because their deeds are clearly seen as evil. There was a time that Jesus walked up to a man that had plenty of demons inside him (Matthews 8:28–34). The Bible states that they knew who he was. How? He was just an ordinary man like you and me. One of Jesus's followers, a man that believed that he has been given the same authority that Jesus has and this same authority he has given to you and me. His name is Peter. Peter in the scriptures was a man that truly believed that he had powers and by faith; he did.

"And believers were the more added to the Lord, multitudes both men and women. Insomuch that they brought forth the sick into the streets and laid them on beds and couches that at least the shadow of Peter passing by, might overshadow some of them. There came also multitudes out of the cities round about unto Jerusalem, binging sick folks, and them which were vexed with unclean spirits; and they were healed [everyone]" (Acts 5:14–16).

The shadow of Peter was the atmosphere of Christ Jesus or GOD Himself. The unclean spirits could not operate in GOD's presence or had zero authority. I believe if they neglected GOD's presence, they would be destroyed through negligence.

I tell you that if you believe that the spirit of GOD is in you, then GOD's authority rules the atmosphere, and you have to believe that. There is no higher authority than GOD's. In order for you to have full power of spirit, you have to carry GOD's agenda that first starts with love toward all men, even the evil.

Both the Father and Jesus have the same mind, and if we take on the mind of Christ and your faith is in GOD Himself, then you, my friend, can have the same power with GOD. His power only functions in Him, or you can say it like this—His power only functions in His plan.

Let me help you with something as we go along. If there is an earthly father that has a son, and that father gives his son permission of his authority to go and accomplish a mission, that father has just released all power to that son. If that son doesn't use that power, it can never be executed. Or if that son doesn't believe that his father would give him that kind of power, then that son would be useless to his father. If he does believe and abuse his power in a plan to accomplish fleshly agenda, he is punished, and there is loss of power as far as heaven and the Holy Spirit is concerned.

Christ Jesus never once abused the Holy Spirit and grieved Him because I've learned that the Holy Spirit will never assist evil. Evil spirits will, but not the Holy Spirit, who is holy. Never grieving the Holy Spirit is how one is exalted in spirit and position with the Father. Jesus was so pleasing to the Father that He is now seated at His right hand. He is now operating directly in the Father's place and in the Father's authority.

You and I are seated with Christ in His authority, executing the same powers under GOD's agenda. "But GOD who is rich in mercy, for His great love where with He loved us. Even when we were dead in sins, hath quickened us together with Christ, by grace ye are saved; and has raised us up together and made us sit together in heavenly places in Christ Jesus" (Ephesians 2:4–6).

If you think on this, there is no evil or human power in GOD's heavenly places, because it is another kingdom. Another rule. Another financial system. Another spirit. Another health. Remember what the scriptures said: "heavenly places."

With GOD, you are either with Him or you are not. What a great privilege to be seated with a man with such great honors. That means that when I speak, GOD speaks, and when I take action, GOD is taking action, and when I walk through this life, GOD is walking through this life. Not that I am GOD myself, because that agenda can bring abuse through negligence of Him. But that I, in His authority by permission through Christ Jesus, am.

We, as the church, must come to this conclusion and learn that heaven's authority is to be separate from all others. Because then we lose power and have to depend on lesser earthly authority. Actions differ from earthly. Our actions should be of Christ Jesus and of the cross. The Holy Spirit of GOD harms no man; the actions of earthly authority given by GOD harms men to execute judgment on evildoers with them included.

Because I've learned that just because GOD gives you an authority does not mean that everything you do or decide GOD agrees. They must be fair and revere the Father, and not themselves. When they revere themselves, that's when abuse occur.

Hitler was ordained by GOD, and so was Saddam Hussein. But these men neglected the GOD of heaven and began to murder men and women from an evil agenda—murdered men and women whose acts were not worthy of death. That's when you see GOD starts to judge, even earthly authority. Because if it was not worthy of death, then it was murder. Because there will be no evildoers in heaven, then there will be no need for these kinds of authorities. That tells us that all earthly authorities must revere the Son of GOD Himself and consider the plan that He has to get all men to heaven.

Through an early death or a death without Christ, GOD loses a soul, and believe it or not, this hurts GOD's heart. That's why heaven's authority only functions from the fruit of the Spirit of GOD. When the church of Jesus Christ does that, they are functioning from one spirit, GOD's.

FOOTSTOOL

In becoming an authority of heaven, some people still won't be in subjection to your authority. In fact, some people may even oppose you. They refused to submit to Jesus. But we don't get angry and fly off the handle like this world. Remember that we deliver the fruit of the Spirit, and we hand it over to the Father. When you hand it over to GOD, He knows how to handle what comes up. Because after all, we are not trying to get them to submit to us, but to Christ Jesus. Once our message is delivered, it now belongs to GOD. It is not our responsibility to force them to obey. Jesus commanded this: "But unto whatsoever city ye enter and they receive you not. Go your ways out into the streets of the same and say, even the very dust of your city, which cleaveth to us, we do wipe off against you; not withstanding that, be sure of this, that the Kingdom of GOD is come nigh unto you" (Luke 10:10–12).

After delivering His message, GOD Himself will come back to see what that city, town, community, or even person has done with that message as far as obedience. He will either bless them by giving them more of Himself and His protection, or He will bring judgment by withdrawing His presence because, after all, it was Him that they rejected, not only the minister. Listen to what the scriptures say about those who reject His message. "But I say unto you, that it will be more tolerable in the day of judgment for Sodom than for that city. The Father has power and authority over this earth" (verse 12). The Bible states that "heaven is His throne and earth is His footstool" (Acts 7:49). We can imagine how sovereign GOD is if His feet rests on this earth. No man can do anything outside of the sight of GOD. I pray that you become an authority of heaven and a child of GOD, the Father.

ABOUT THE AUTHOR

Marco was born a southern Methodist, fifty miles north of New Orleans, in the city of Hammond, Louisiana. When he got older, he decided to be a nondenominational Christian because he believed in eliminating all distractions and religious beliefs that seek to take away the authority and focus of Jesus Christ. Eventually, all true believers will come to one union of the One True God.

www.ingramcontent.com/pod-product-compliance
Lightning Source LLC
LaVergne TN
LVHW020422080526
838202LV00055B/5000